The Negro Motorist Green Book: 1947

restored and reprinted by

New York History Review 2022

Elmira, New York

The Negro Motorist Green Book: 1947

By Victor H. Green, originally published 1947, restored and reprinted by New York History Review in 2022.

For more information www.NewYorkHistoryReview.com

ISBN: 978-1-950822-22-5

Printed in the United States of America.

THE Negro Motorist GREEN BOOK

INTRODUCTION

The idea of "The Green Book" is to give the Motorist and tourist a Guide not only of the Hotels and Tourist Homes in all of the large cities, but other classifications that will be found useful wherever he may be. Also facts and information that the Negro Motorist can use and depend upon.

There are thousands of places that the public doesn't know about and aren't listed. Perhaps you might know of some? If so, send in their names and addresses and the kind of business, so that we might pass it along to the rest of your fellow Motorists.

You will find it handy on your travels, whether at home or in some other state, and is up to date. Each year we are compiling new lists as some of these places move, or go out of business and new business places are started giving added employment to members of our race.

When you are traveling mention "The Green Book" so as to let these people know just how you found out about their place of business. If they haven't heard about This Guide, tell them to get in touch with us.

If this Guide is useful, let us know, if not tell us also, as we appreciate your criticisms.

If any errors are found, kindly notify the publishers so that they can be corrected in the next issue.

Publication Office—Leonia, N. J.—Victor H. Green, Editor.
Published yearly by Victor H. Green & Co.
Advertising Office—200 West 135th St., Room 215-A, New York City, N. Y.
Copyrighted—1947 by Victor H. Green. Manuscripts submitted for publication should be sent to 200 West 135th St., Room 215-A, New York 30, N. Y., and must be accompanied by return postage. No liability can be assumed for the loss or damage to manuscripts although every possible precaution will be taken.
District Advertising Representative:—
Western Representative—Elmer Jackson-2605 Euclid Ave., Kansas City, Mo.
Subscription: Seventy Five cents per copy.
Advertising: For rates, Write to the publisher.
Last forms close on Nov. 1st. We reserve the right to reject any advertising which in our opinion does not conform to our standards.

PHOTO CREDIT—(Cover.) Maine Development Comm. "Orr's Island" to the Mainland

INDEX

EXPLANATION

No travel guide is complete with the multitude of business places that are unheard of. The principal value is its completeness for which reason we are endeavoring to make this guide actually the most complete possible.

We have given you a selection of listings that you might choose from, under no circumstances do these listings imply that the place is recommended.

The business classifications listed have been arranged under the different cities and towns, so that one won't have any trouble finding what they want.

MONEY FOR NEGRO COLLEGES

This year more than ever we must see to it that our colleges are prepared to carry a maximum load of work, and ready to do it well. One group of colleges deserves special attention in this respect: the institutions that devote themselves to education of the Negro. Under the leadership of the United Negro College Fund thirty-three of these private colleges are beginning a campaign for $1,300,000. John D. Rockefeller Jr. is chairman of the advisory committee for this third annual fund drive, and a number of other prominent men and women have interested themselves in the cause.

The need for full subscription is more pressing this year because of the unusual burden thrown on all educational facilities by the returning veteran. The Negro played an important and often heroic part in the war. He shared the mud, the danger, the sweat and the tears. Now he has the right to continue his interrupted education if he wants to do so. Many college doors will be closed to him, and to others regardless of race, color or creed, simply because there are too many returning veterans to be cared for at once in the colleges of their choice. But we cannot allow these thirty-three Negro private colleges to turn away any applicant because they lack funds, or to curtail their programs because of it.

The educated Negro was once a rarity. His numbers are increasing year by year, and his contributions to the arts, science and education steadily gain a wider and juster recognition for his abilities. From these we all gain, regardless of color. And, as we mutually put a proper, unprejudiced estimate on the contributions of all races to the common good, we move surely closer to the goal of living together in harmony.

REPRINTED WITH PERMISSION OF THE N. Y. TIMES

Negro Schools and Colleges in the United States

Just a few pages ahead you will find a list of Negro schools and colleges in the United States.

As you visit the various states you will have a splendid opportunity of visiting the great educational centers, where students receive a sound, enlightened humanistic education and where they are prepared for life with a fine linguistic equipment, a trained ability to examine facts critically, a sharpened and heightened sensibility to values, a developed capacity for historical and philosophical reflection, and as a culminative result of all these disciplines, an enhanced capacity for reflective decision and action.

Take time out to read or to see these great homes of learning where the young folks of today and tomorrow are having their characters moulded. Plan for the future of your children so that in time to come they will face life with a fine equipment. Let us not forget that with this question of schools the whole of education is bound up, for the greatest thought of mankind is in books and the greatest living teachers are in our schools and colleges in the United States.

ERNESTINE L. HOPPS, Director

"Negro Schools and Colleges in the United States"

ALABAMA

Birmingham
Miles Memorial College

Huntsville
Oakwood College

Selma
Selma University

Montgomery
State Teachers College

Tuscaloosa
Stillman Institute

Talladega
Talladega College

Tuskegee
Tuskegee Normal and
Industrial Institute

ARKANSAS

Pine Bluff
Agricultural Mechanical, and
Normal College

Little Rock
Arkansas Baptist College
Dunbar Junior College
Philander Smith College

North Little Rock
Shorter College

DELAWARE

Dover
State College for Colored
Students

DISTRICT OF COLUMBIA

Washington
Howard University
Miner Teachers College

FLORIDA

Daytona Beach
Bethune-Cookman College

Jacksonville
Edward Waters College

St. Augustine
Florida Normal and Industrial
Institute

Tallahassee
Florida Agricultural and
Mechanical College

GEORGIA

Atlanta
Atlanta School of Social Work
Atlanta University
Morehouse College
Spelman College
Clark University
Gammon Theological Seminary
Morris Brown University

Albany
Georgia Normal and Agricultural
College

Augusta
Paine College

Fort Valley
Fort Valley Normal and
Industrial School

Industrial College
Georgia State College

KENTUCKY

Frankfort
Kentucky State Industrial
College

Louisville
Louisville Municipal College for
Negroes

LOUISIANA

New Orleans
Dillard University
Xavier University

Baker
Leland College

Grambling
Louisiana Normal and
Industrial Institute

Scotlandville
Southern University and Agricultural and Mechanical College

MARYLAND

Baltimore
Morgan College
Coppin Normal School
Bowie
Maryland State Teachers College
Princess Anne
Princess Anne College

MISSISSIPPI

Alcorn
Alcorn Agricultural and
Mechanical College
Jackson
Campbell College
Jackson College
Holly Springs
Rust College
Edwards
Southern Christian Institute
Tougaloo
Tougaloo College

MISSOURI

Jefferson City
Lincoln University
St. Louis
Stowe Teachers College

NORTH CAROLINA

Greensboro
Bennett College
Fayetteville
Fayetteville State Normal
School
Charlotte
Johnson C. Smith University
Salisbury
Livingstone College
Greensboro
Agricultural and Technical
College
Durham
North Carolina State College

Raleigh
Shaw University
Elizabeth City
State Teachers College
Winston-Salem
Winston-Salem Teachers College

OHIO

Wilberforce
Wilberforce University

OKLAHOMA

Langston
Agricultural and Normal
University

PENNSYLVANIA

Cheyney
Cheynly Training School for
Teachers
Lincoln University
Lincoln University

SOUTH CAROLINA

Columbia
Allen University
Charleston
Avery Institute
Columbia
Benedict College
Trenton
Bettis Academy
Chester
Brainerd Junior College
Orangeburg
Clafflin College
Rock Hill
Clinton Normal and Industrial
Institute
Cheraw
Coulter Memorial Academy
Rock Hill
Friendship College
Sumter
Morris College

Seneca
  Seneca Junior College

Orangeburg
  State Normal, Industrial, Agricultural and Mechanical College

Denmark
  Voorhees Normal and Industrial School

TENNESSEE

Nashville
  Fisk University

Knoxville
  Knoxville College

Jackson
  Lane College

Memphis
  Le Moyne College

Nashville
  Meharry Medical College

Morristown
  Morristown Normal and Industrial College

Rogersville
  Swift Memorial Junior College

Nashville
  Tennessee Agricultural and Industrial State Teachers College

TEXAS

Marshall
  Bishop College

Tyler
  Butler College

Seguin
  Guadalupe College

Houston
  Houton College for Negroes

Hawkins
  Jarvis Christian College

Crockett
  Mary Allen Junior College

Waco
  Paul Quinn College

Prairie View
  Prairie View State College

San Antonio
  St. Philip's Junior College and Vocational Institute

Austin
  Samuel Houton College

Tyler
  Texas College

Austin
  Tillotson

Marshall
  Wiley College

VIRGINIA

Petersburg
  Bishop Payne Divinity School

Hampton
  Hampton Institute

Suffolk
  Nansemond Collegiate Institute

Lawrenceville
  St. Paul Normal and Industrial School

Ettrick
  Virginia State College

Lynchburg
  Virginia Theological Seminary and College

Richmond
  Virginia Union University

WEST VIRGINIA

Bluefield
  Bluefield State Teachers College

Harpers Ferry
  Storer College

Institute
  West Virginia State College

Leading Negro Publications of the United States

Listed below are the countries leading newspapers. When you reach your destination, from the list below, purchase a copy of their paper and enjoy the latest news from all over the world.

ALABAMA
Birmingham
  Newspic Magazine
  Weekly Review
Gadsden
  Call Post
Mobile
  Gulf Informer
Montgomery
  Alabama Tribune
Tuscaloosa
  Alabama Black Citizen

ARKANSAS
Hot Springs
  Crusader Journal
Little Rock
  Arkansas Survey Journal .
  State Press
  Arkansas World
Pine Bluff
  Negro Spokesman

CALIFORNIA
Los Angeles
  California Eagle
  Sentinel
  Tribune
Oakland
  California Voice

COLORADO
Denver
  Colorado Statesman
  Star
  Pueblo Western Ideal

DISTRICT OF COLUMBIA
Washington
  Afro-American
  Tribune

FLORIDA
Jacksonville
  Florida Tattler
Miami
  Florida Times
  Whip
Pensacola
  Courier
  Junior Press
Tampa
  Bulletin

GEORGIA
Albany
  Enterprise
Atlanta
  World Syndicate
  World
Augusta
  Echo
Columbus
  World
Rome
  Enterprise
Savannah
  Tribune

ILLINOIS
Champaign
  Illinois Times
Chicago
  Bee
  Defender
Springfield
  Illinois Conservator

INDIANA
Gary
  American
Indianapolis
  Recorder

7

IOWA
Des Moines
   Iowa Bystander
   Iowa Observer

KANSAS
Kansas City
   Plaindealer
Wichita
   Negro Star

KENTUCKY
Louisville
   Defender
   Leader

LOUISIANA
New Orleans
   Informer-Sentinel
   Louisiana Weekly
   Sepia Socialite
Shreveport
   Sun

MARYLAND
Baltimore
   Afro-American

MASSACHUSETTS
Boston
   Chronicle
   Times

MICHIGAN
Detroit
   Michigan Chronicle
   Tribune

MINNESOTA
Minneapolis
   Spokesman
St. Paul
   Recorder

MISSISSIPPI
Greenville
   Delta Leader

Jackson
   Advocate
Meridan
   Weekly Echo

MISSOURI
Jefferson City
   Lincoln Clarion
Kansas City
   Call
St. Louis
   American
   Argus

NEBRASKA
Omaha
   Guide
   Star

NEW JERSEY
Newark
   New Jersey Afro-American
   New Jersey Herald-News
   Record

NEW YORK
Buffalo
   The Star
New York
   Age
   Amsterdam News
   Crisis
   Music Dial (Magazine)
   Peoples' Voice
Syracuse
   Progressive (Herald)

NORTH CAROLINA
Durham
   Carolina Times
Raleigh
   Carolinian
Wilmington
   Cape Fear Journal

OHIO

Cincinnati
  Independent

Cleveland
  Call & Post

Columbus
  Ohio State News

Dayton
  Bulletin
  Dayton-Cincinnati Forum

Youngstown
  Buckeye Review

OKLAHOMA

Muskogee
  Oklahoma Independent

Oklahoma City
  Black Dispatch

Tulsa
  Oklahoma Eagle

PENNSYLVANIA

Philadelphia
  Afro-American
  Christian Review
  Independent
  Tribune

Pittsburg
  Courier

RHODE ISLAND

Providence
  Chronicle

SOUTH CAROLINA

Columbia
  Lighthouse and Informer
  Palmetto Leader

TENNESSEE

Chattanooga
  Observer

Knoxville
  Flashlight Herald

Memphis
  World

Nashville
  Globe & Independent
  National Baptist Union Review

TEXAS

Dallas
  Express

Fort Worth
  Mind

Galveston
  Voice

Houston
  Defender
  Informer
  Negro Labor News

San Antonio
  Informer
  Register

Waco
  Messenger

VIRGINIA

Norfolk
  Journal and Guide

Richmond
  Afro-American

Roanoke
  Tribune

WASHINGTON

Seattle
  Northwest Enterprise

WEST VIRGINIA

Charleston
  West Virginia Digest
  Color Magazine

Not only Happy Motoring
But Happy Travelling by any method, is obtainable
through Green Book Routing
Say the ESSO Special Representatives

Editors Note:-The following article is as nearly as is possible, a reproduction of a discussion between Wendall P. Alston and James A. Jackson, both Special Representatives of the Esso Marketers.

JAMES A. JACKSON, the senior has attempted to reproduce his reactions to the book and its field of usefulness, by reminiscing a bit about his early travels. In the pursuit of a livlihood since the dawn of the century, Mr. Jackson has covered a lot of territory. He has actually visited 1997 towns and cities in the United States and on several trips abroad has been in Nineteen foreign countries. He has been in so many communities in America as to be quite at home in most of them, because of his frequent visits, as time went on.

His present position, held for the past twelve years, after seven years in the U. S. Dept. of Commerce and six with the Billboard, a theatrical magazine is with the Public Relations Department of the Standard Oil Co. and its affiliated companies. Mr. W. P. Alston has for the past two years been his traveling companion, and his potential successor. Together they go about to the extent of around 20,000 miles per year.

But let them tell their own story:-

When this article reaches print in the 1947 issue of the Green Book, the authors of this little brochure will be wandering down in Louisiana, and Arkansas; and in fact one of us will have been across the border and into Texas. For about six weeks beginning right after Xmas, we will be on a trip of more than three thousand miles, involving fourteen stops in each state.

Both of us are experienced travellers and one is especially fortified with contacts in many towns and cities which he has been visiting at intervals for, in some instances, more than forty years. The gray headed member of the team, whose experiences indicate his age, but whose energy and will to get about this and other countries, seems to be undiminished.

Of course, like all old codgers, he is inclined to reminisce at almost any opportunity. Talk of the Green Book and mention of comparisons since its first publication a scant half dozen years ago, has just set him off.

"Gee" said he, "If there had been any such publication as this when I started travelling 'way back in the Nineties, I would have missed a lot of anxieties, worries and saved a lot of mental energy which, had it been conserved and used solely to the advancement of the business interests for which I traveled, my years "on the road' might have been concluded long ago, with enough savings to permit my living a life of peace and quiet, now that I am becoming an old codger."

JAMES A. JACKSON (SEATED) AND WENDEL P. ALSTON, SPECIAL REPRESENTATIVES OF THE ESSO MARKETERS IN THEIR NEW YORK OFFICE.

Of course, he could not be stopped traveling any more than one could stop him from talking about "Back when;" but make no mistake about his yarns, they are factual experiences and one, by one, as we go about, somewhere we encounter people familiar with the incident, or incidents, about which he has talked at sometime or another.

"When I first started jumping from place to place, just like white commercial travellers have been doing for time immemorial" he continued; the folk in many, many places looked with fear and doubt upon the traveling man from beyond the borders of their own county. In like manner, I, said he "wondered if my bags were safe, and if the bed I acquired for the night would be mine alone; or if I would have the night companions such as those for which D. D. T. has been created."

11

Hotels, such as they were had been designed solely as a place for the too inebriated man to occupy rather than to go home to an angry spouse in his unfortunate condition, according to the elder of this team. At other places, the doors were innocent of locks; and much of the equipment for bathrooms, such as are common place today, were unknown where Negro travellers might stop. It seems that the major bit of bathroom equipment could be found anywhere from fifty to a hundred feet down the yard and on the way, a grape arbor afforded the only shelter from storm.

Slowly the more modern hotels conducted for our patronage came into being during the past four or five decades, and as slowly, or even more slowly, have the minds of the owners and managers of these improved institutions of comfort and service, realized that to obtain patronage, the Negroes of the country must be informed of heir existence.

How much nicer it is today, when one in contemplating a trip by train, motor or plane, is able to have determined in advance the places he may stop at while in the different communities; and how much more is the peace of mind of the traveller; and of his family and associates left at home, knowing that in emergency, just where one may be found.

I believe the Green Book was created in response to growing auto tourist business that would support it. However, what difference does it make to the traveller, or to the hotel and tourist home keeper, about what means of travel may be involved. The traveller needs a "home away from home" to the profit of those who make such homes available.

Just in case some of the Green Book readers may identify us form either the pictures or recognize the owner of the gray head from his talk as quoted here, Jack reminds the editor that "I am broad minded enough to want the traveler by train and plane to enjoy their stops anywhere just the same as if they had traveled by car. I am broad minded that way: and besides, Planes use petroleum products for motive power, so do a lot of railway engines, and all of them have to have lubrication, so my employer is not being cheated too badly, not enough to warrant them having an objection to all travelling colored people being able to obtain some degree of peace and comfort when they go away from home regardless of how they travel.

They're nice that way, therefore those who may be motoring may express their gratitude to Mr. Green for making possible the serenity of the trip; and insure themselves of Happy motoring by using Esso products while on tour, thereby adding to the writers a degree of Job insurance and enhance the social security of our families as they enjoy Happy motoring with ESSO.

GENERAL MOTORS CARS

At the time our guide went to press the 1947 Models of
General Motors Cars had not been announced.

CHEVROLET

The new Chevrolet uses the valve-in-head Thrift-Master engine famous for its rare combination of economy and performance. This engine extracts more power from a given quantity of fuel than do other types of engines of the same displacement. Durability and ease of servicing also are important advantages of the valve-in-head construction.

Chevrolet alone, among the lowest-priced cars, has the famous Body by Fisher and all that it provides in styling, safety comfort, luxury, and durability. A distinctive feature of this body is its steel construction. The thoroughly reinforced cowl, side, rear, and floor panels and Turret Top are welded to form an all-steel unit of tremendous strength.

Still another Chevrolet feature is a vacuum cylinder which does nearly all of the gear shifting work. All the driver has to do is move the lever and the lever works so easy that you can move it with your forefinger without taking your hand off the steering wheel. You shift the gears but not your grip.

PONTIAC

Your first impression of the big, new Pontiac is that here is a car of outstanding beauty. Its clean, sweeping lines accentuate its length and size. Every detail of design adds to its stunning beauty. But its extra value is even more evident when you open the wide doors and get a glimpse of the luxurious interior. Here again, every detail of appointment adds up to comfort and luxury unmatched in its price class, and gives you the beauty of custom-type appointments at low cost.

Pontiac interiors are roomy, comfortable and in trim good taste. Soft, pleasing colors and smart hardware combine with plenty of elbow and headroom to add to passenger comfort. Upholstery is rich and luxurious. Ash trays and built-in arm rests are another "plus value" feature of all Pontiac models.

Pontiac's reputation for trouble-free performance is the result of advanced engineering and good craftsmanship. From drawing board to assembly line, Pontiac is designed and built to give mile after mile of trouble-free, economical performance, as the experience of owners has proved over and over again.

Many Pontiacs have been driven 100,000 miles and more with unbelievably little care and expense. New mechanical improvements combined with scores of time-proved features prove that in operating economy and dependability the 1946 Pontiac brings new perfection to its price class.

Oldsmobile "98" 4 Door Sedan

OLDSMOBILE

Ever since the days of the "Curved Dash Runabout," Oldsmobile has been famous for combining new ideas with proved features . . .in the right proportion to create a fine automobile. This tradition is carried out in the new Oldsmobiles.

Yet it takes the experience of actually driving the Oldsmobile to gain a real appreciation of how it combines many new improvements—in engine and body and chassis—with proved quality features and basic soundness of design. Add to these advantages the New Hydra-Matic Drive—the famous General Motors feature that gives you fully automatic gear-shifting and eliminates the clutch pedal entirely.

Built for the owner who wants quality construction plus outstanding economy, the Oldsmobile Special is a roomy, roadworthy automobile, offering many unusual extra-value features. The 1946 Oldsmobile Special "66" is 204 inches long overall—a full 17 feet from bumper to bumper. Its wheelbase is 119 inches. Its precision-balanced Fire-Power Engine delivers 100 horsepower. And this fine economy car is a true Oldsmobile through and through —in styling, in engineering, and in every detail of construction.

The Custom 8 Cruiser is truly the finest Oldsmobile ever built, a car for the owner who demands the finest in styling, in comfort, and in performance. It is a big impressive-looking car, 18 feet long from bumper to bumper, with a wheelbase of 127 inches It is a modern car, with floors so low that running boards are not needed, and with bodies that are

14

wider than they are high. It is a luxurious car, with custom-quality appointments and DeLuxe equipment throughout. And this fine big Oldsmobile is so perfectly balanced that it is one of the easiest-handling cars on the road. Beneath its broad hood is a 110-horsepower "Straight 8" Engine, with outstanding new features that contribute to new standards of smoothness and performance.

BUICK

Buick's line includes the Special, Series 40; the Super, Series 50; and the Roadmaster, Series 70. Here we picture the interior of Model 51, the sleek, clean-lined four-door SUPER sedan.

In many instances in this 1946 Buick Fireball valve-in-head engine, parts are held to closer tolerances than in precision power plants of the air.

There's a closer fit between the pistons and the cylinder walls than in an aircraft engine. There's quieter action because of closer fits in the valve mechanism.

Connecting rods ride on crankshaft bearings more closely fitted to journals. Oil pump gears mesh more precisely. Camshaft bearings meet closer standards of fit.

This all means extra fine, smooth performance and longer engine life. And this meticulous matching is only part of the whole Buick engine story.

There is the valve-in-head principle with the Dynaflash combustion chamber which rolls the fuel into a power-packed charge, squeezes it into a flattened ball so that it lets go with a super-stout wallop.

Yes, this Buick Fireball straight-eight for 1946 is a great engine. More brilliantly agile, more frugal with fuel and oil, and definitely proof that "When Better Automobiles Are Built Buick Will Build Them."

CADILLAC

First among automobile companies, Cadillac was singled out by the government for war production. During those war years when no civilian cars were produced, Cadillac's precision workmanship continued uninterrupted . . . the Cadillac engine and transmission assembly lines never stopped. Cadillac's contribution to Victory remained, to a large extent, in the familiar realm of automotive-type production.

Naturally, automotive progress went far ahead at Cadillac. Over 50,000 of the famous Cadillac V-type engines and Hydra-Matic transmissions went into tanks and other motorized weapons . . . met the grueling tests of the battlefields . . . to emerge toughened and hardened to new standards of efficiency and dependability. Their development was far greater than would have been possible during four peacetime years.

This new mechanical perfection of engine and Hydra-Matic transmission is but one reflection of how Cadillac is able to resume fine car production with the most advanced new cars in

This is Cadillac's 62 Model

its distinguished history . . . why the new, Cadillac is the greatest of all time, improved even beyond expectations.

In this basic mechanical improvement alone is the assurance that Cadillac—whose leadership long ago established its cars as "Standard of the World"—again today is creating fine cars which advance comfort, luxury and automotive performance to a new, far higher standard.

Facts on Future Automotive Design

APPEARANCE

Henry Ford II has said that new cars, meaning the 1947 models, will be "evolutionary" and not "revolutionary." There won't be any radical changes although the '47 models will certainly feature more changes than any previous models in company history. In general, however, the trend is toward smoother, aerodynamically clean lines.

RIDE

Cars of the future will provide progressively better rides. Possibilities for suspension include: torsion bars, rubber, air, oil, conventional and coil spring arrangements. Whatever is used, the motorist can count on getting an increasingly smoother ride from his motor car.

TIRES

According to Mr. James, natural rubber tires should not be counted out. There is much to recommend them. At the present time, they are not only cheaper, but easier on gasoline. Experiments show that they enable the motorist to get at least an extra mile to the gallon.

There is no evidence that synthetic tires, at present, last longer than the natural product.

Big synthetic winner is the butyl rubber inner tube. Due to less porosity they have much better air retention properties.

ENGINES

Mr. James feels that the conventional, reciprocating engine is still the best power source available for the present automobile. He sees lighter, more compact engines creating far greater horsepower for a given displacement. He is not so sure compressions will go much higher. Higher compressions, he says, impose greater strains on bearings, create higher temperatures, result in a "high strung" or tempermental engine in frequent need of attention.

He says there is a possibility the same end—greater horsepower for a given displacement and weight—may be achieved by the use of superchargers.

According to Mr. James, gas turbines as power plants for "tomorrow's" automobiles leave much to be desired—at least in their present stage of development. He says they have a bright future in the heavy power plant field, i. e. airplanes, sea-going vessels, trains and special power plants requiring 1,000 or more horsepower.

Advantages of the gas turbine are: compactness, fewer-moving parts, low initial cost and weight, ability to use low volatile fuels. Chief disadvantages are: Higher fuel consumption and their inability, in the present state of development, to be produced satisfactorily as small power units.

TRANSMISSIONS

Mr. James says that "easier to shift" transmissions are on their way. Clutch pedals are likely to disappear on all models in the near future. He is not sure that the gear shift lever will disappear entirely, although smaller, easier-to-manage levers are definitely in the picture. The matter of selectivity is something motorists must decide. Do they want a transmission that is fully automatic or do they want to exercise some choice in the matter? Semi-automatic and fully automatic transmissions are already a reality.

FUELS

The cars of the future will determine the kind of fuel we get according to Mr. James. He points out that a car lasts seven years; a fuel only seven weeks from refinery to engine.

LIGHT METAL AND PLASTICS

There is little likelihood of an aluminum, magnesium or all plastic automobile in the future, says Mr. James. Chief trouble with aluminum is that it is too expensive. It now costs from 15 to 16 cents a pound. The industry will get interested when it gets down to 4 or 5 cents. This seems unlikely since it takes two cents of electricity to make a pound of the meatl.

On the other hand the present cost of steel is around 2 cents a pound.

Fabricating problems of aluminum could be licked, Mr. James believes. It's a matter of basic cost that is the stumbling block.

The plastics picture is the same as aluminum or magnesium. Basic costs are high, and in addition there is a higher cost of fabrication to consider.

REAR ENGINE DRIVE AND FRONT ENGINE DRIVE

Prme advantages of either of these arrangements, Mr. James says, is that both permit lower floors. This is an important design consideration. He forsees considerable experimentation with both in the near future.

A secondary advantage of the rear engine design, one not possessed by the front drive, is improved visibility.

Problems of rear engine desgns are: weight distribution difficulties and cooling.

AIR CONDITIONING

There is a good chance that motor cars in the near future may feature controlled year-around temperature, obviating the necessity for opening the windows at any time. Humidity, too, will be controlled, eliminating interior fogging.

THE FORD CAR

At the time our guide went to press the 1947 Ford Motors Cars had not been announced.

Ford's New Sportsman's Convertible

Seven reasons why the Ford Motor Company's new Sportsman's Convertible combines custom craftsmanship with production cost are shown here.

Outstanding feature of the Sportsman's convertible is the use of wood panels on a steel frame, combining strength with station wagon appeal.

Examining the new model at Dearborn are seven of the nation's outstanding custom automobile designers, all of whom have recently joined Ford's expanded styling department. They are, left to right:

John F. Dobben, formerly with J. B. Judkins Company, Merrimac, Mass., builders of custom bodies for Lincoln, Pierce-Arrow, Packard, Deusenberg, and other luxury cars. He designed special bodies for Tom Mix, W. C. Fields and other screen notables.

Tom Hibbard, formerly of Hibbard and Darrin, Paris France. Hibbard's firm built custom bodies for Rolls Royce, Packard, Lincoln, Mercedes, Renault, Hispano Suiza, Pierce-Arrow, Isotta-Frachinni and othr famed con- Deusenberg for ex-King Alphonso of tinental makes. He designed a special Spain.

Martin Regitko, formerly with the Willoughby Company of Utica, N. Y., custom body builders for Lincoln, Rolls Royce, Deusenberg and others. He helped design special cars for presidents including Coolidge and Hoover. All were built on Lincoln chassis.

George Tasman, designer for Locke & Company, and J. S. Inkskip, both of New York. The latter was agent for Rolls Royce and Bentley. He has designed scores of custom bodies.

Herman Brunn, son and partner of Herman A. Brunn, of Brunn & Company, Buffalo. He was stylist and designer for his father and later for Kellner and Company, Paris France. He once designed an all-white ceremonial car with solid gold trim for the Shah of Iran.

Victor Lang, formerly with Brunn and Company, custom body builders for Lincoln, Pierce-Arrow, Rolls Royce and other. He designed a special Lincoln body on a 150-inch ambulance chassis for the late President Roosevelt. The car now is being used by President Truman.

Paul Weichbrodt, formerly with Willoughby and Brunn of Utica, N. Y., custom body designers for many notables, including numerous film stars.

The 1946 Ford is not a "stop-gap" model hurriedly produced but is the result of four years of research and production know-how, Ford Motor Company officials said today.

The 1946 Ford is designed and built without compromise of traditional Ford quality in workmanship and material. It contains more mechanical improvements than were included in any previous year to year model.

Outstanding features of the car are: a more powerful engine, better performance, longer life, improved economy and a better ride.

The new V-8 engine develops 100 horsepower, making it the most powerful Ford in the history of the company. Pre-war Fords were equipped with V-8 engines developing 90 horsepower.

The chief exterior change is a newly designed radiator grille. The louvres are fewer in number and larger. They

1946 Super De Luxe Fordor

20

extend horizontally from fender to fender, enhancing a lower, broader appearance.

Other exterior changes include a new hood ornament and a more elaborate rear deck ornamentation. In addition a complete line of colors will be available in the long-wearing, durable Ford synthetic enamel paints.

Luxury and eye-appeal are accentuated in the interiors. Instrumentation is generally the same, but the styling and color schemes of the instrument panel are new.

Upholstery will be available in mohair-broadcloth of several shades. Imitation wood grain panels have given way to subdued panels that blend into the general interior color scheme.

Durable, eye-appealing art-leather decorates the door panels and interior trim.

An improved ride and better roadability, especially at high speeds in cross winds or on curves is assured by the use of improved-type springs and shock absorbers and the addition of a rear-end sway bar.

The thickness of the spring leaves has been reduced and their number increased.

Shock absorbers have improved oil seals to prevent loss of fluid.

The brakes also have received considerable attention. They are new and require less pedal pressure. They are easier to adjust and feature a floating type shoe that seats itself.

A Lincoln-type hand brake lever has been adopted as standard equipment on all Ford Models.

Radiator brackets have been redesigned to prevent radiator corners from breaking and causing leakage. In addition, the hood latch has been changed to a stamping to eliminate possibility of breakage.

Other improvements are: the use of self-locking nuts wherever possible to eliminate the necessity for using cotter pins; a tool bag that is made from artificial leather in place of burlap, and a car jack of ratchet type design. The latter replaces the friction type formerly used.

Improved cooling has been achieved by the adoption of a new radiator pressure cap that maintains a constant pressure of five pounds inside the radiator. Evaporation is reduced and winter anti-freeze preserved. Ford is first in the low-priced field to incorporate this feature in regular production.

Aluminum pistons equipped with four rings will be standard on all models. This, coupled with an improved rear main bearing seal, will effect further economies in oil consumption and prevent loss.

A new standard in fuel economy has been achieved despite an increase in horsepower. Higher engine compression, a change in the engine-axle ratio and the adoption of a new carburetor has made this possible.

Longer life for the camshaft timing gear has been obtained by changing over to aluminum.

A newly designed distributor virtually eliminates possibility of motor interference or stoppage resulting from condensation or water seepage. The use of oil repellant and long lasting Neoprene covering for ignition wires has eliminated another troublesome feature of pre-war motoring.

All Ford models will feature oil bath air and oil cleaners as standard equipment, wartime use of these accessories having demonstrated their value in prolonging engine life.

Valves on the new engines have been moved outward form the cylinders permitting improved water jacketing and better cooling. Intake and exhaust valves have been equipped with hardened, heat-resisting alloy steel inserts to save the cost of adjustments and regrinding. Using inserts for both intake and exhaust valves is an exclusive Ford feature.

Cylinder block heads for new V-8 engines have been made interchangeable, requiring a change in gasket design.

Possibility of over heating under adverse conditions has been dealt another blow by the development of a new oil pump that circulates a greater volume of oil through the engine lubrication system at a higher pressure.

Valve springs are shot-peened and rust proofed for longer life. The main leaf on each spring is also shot-peened for added strength.

As in the past, sturdy, high-torque Ford 6-cylinder engines well be available for those who prefer the in-line type.

A number of changes have been made in this rugged engine, thousands of which power various military vehicles.

Like the V-8, the new 6-cylinder engine features aluminum pistons and 4 rings for greater oil economy, the new improved distributor, oil filter and oil filtered air cleaner. It also has shot-peened and rust-proofed valve springs and a number of other features incorporated on the larger engine.

In addition new front motor supports have been added. These are made from Neoprene, a synthetic product that is unaffected by oil.

The exhaust manifold has been re-designed so that it is removed far enough from the fuel pump to eliminate possibility of vapor lock.

General engine performance of the Ford 6 has been stepped up by the use of a new, higher lift cam. It develops 90 horsepower at 3300 rpm.

THE 1946 MERCURY

DETROIT, Mich.,—The 1946 Mercury, according to Frank J. Denney, general sales manager for the Lincoln-Mercury Division of the Ford Motor Company, has a heavier, lower and wider appearance, resulting from a wider hood and re-designed front grille.

The new grille consists of die-cast, vertical louvres extending across the

1946 Mercury Two Door Sedan

front. The lines of the hood ornament also have been changed to connote fleetness and beauty.

Separate "Mercury" and "Eight" nameplates have been added, and mouldings have been widened all around the car to accentuate the length and low center of gravity.

The new Mercury is available in eight exterior colors, with harmonizing instrument panels, upholstery and trim.

Two distinctive interior treatments are used. One features gray-green broadcloth upholstery and a modernistic gray-green lacquered instrument panel with contrasting plastic trim. Doors are paneled with gray-green art leather.

The other interior features rust brown cord upholstery with a golden brown lacquered instrument panel and brown art leather paneling on the doors.

Engineering knowledge gained during research and production of wartime goods is reflected in the mechanical changes incorporated in the 1946 Mercury engine.

These include such outstanding features as tri-alloy bearings, crank-case ventilation, improved oil pump, four-ring aluminum pistons, and interchangeable cylinder heads.

Riding comfort in the new Mercury has been increased through redesigning of the springs. The spring leaves are thinner and their number has been increased.

A track bar has been added in the rear, to prevent "wander" on the road in high winds, and a floating-shoe brake has been developed. Brake pedal

1946 Lincoln

IN PATRONIZING THESE PLACES

pressure is softer, increasing driving comfort.

The wheelbase is 118 inches.

Mr. Denney has announced that plans are progressing for establishment of an exclusive Mercury dealer organization, as well as separation of production facilities. Prior to the war, Mercury cars were merchandised largely through the Ford dealer organization.

Assembly locations for the post-war Mercury will include the three plants of the Lincoln Division—the Detroit Lincoln plant at Warren and Livernois, and the two new Lincoln-Mercury plants now under construction on the East and West coasts.

THE 1946 LINCOLN

Detroit, Mich.-The 1946 Lincoln was the first of the post-war luxury automobiles to be shown to the public in dealer showrooms throughout the nation.

According to Frank J. Denney, general sales manager, the new model retains the graceful lines first introduced to the quality field by Lincoln, but a number of improvements give the cars a larger and more luxurious appearance.

Exterior improvements include wider bumpers, to provide more protection for fenders, and completely new bumper guards, heavier at the top to prevent override and possible damage to fenders and grille.

The new grille, a massive die-casting with a quadrated pattern, gives the front a lower, broader appearance, and provision for built-in fog lights is a new safety feature that adds an attractive note as well.

Electrically operated hydraulic mechanism, for raising and lowering windows is a standard feature on all 1946 Lincoln cars. This is more convenient and safer than the conventional mechanism, since the driver can, with the pressure of one finger, raise or lower either of the car's front windows at any time.

Mr. Denney said that, with new grilles, new bumpers, new color combinations, new rich upholstery, new hardware throughout, new panel instruments, new steering wheel and automatic window lifts, the new Lincoln is by all odds the most beautiful and finest automobile yet offered the American public.

Two models of the 1946 Lincoln are now in production, the four-door sedan and the club coupe, with other models to be added soon. The new Lincolns will be available in eight different exterior colors.

Prices for the 1946 Lincolns, as announced by OPA are:

F. O. B. Detroit—Club Coupe, $1,986. 40; Club Coupe with custom interior, $2,112.28; Four-Door Sedan, $2,002.65 and Sedan with custom interior, $2,128.55. These prices include state and federal taxes, gasoline and oil.

ALABAMA

ANNISTON

HOTELS
St. Thomas—127 W. 10th St.

ANDALUSIA

TOURIST HOMES
Mrs. Ed. Andrews—69 Cotton St.

BIRMINGHAM

HOTELS
Dunbar—323 N. 17th St.
Palm Leaf—328½ N. 18th St.
Rush—316 N. 18th St.
New Home—1718½—4th Ave.

GADSDEN

TOURISTS HOMES
Mrs. A. Sheperd—1324 4th Ave.
Mrs. J. Simons—233 N. 6th St.

GENEVA

TOURISTS HOMES
Joe Dondal
Susie M. Sharp

MOBILE

TOURISTS HOMES
E. Reed—950 Lyons St.
E. Jordan—256 N. Dearborn St.
F. Wildins 254 N. Dearborn St.
BEAUTY PARLORS
Ritz—607 Congress St.

MONTGOMERY

HOTELS
Douglass—121 Monroe Ave.
Royal Palm—109 Monore Ave.
RESTAURANTS
Bonnie's—390 W. Jeff Davis Ave.
TAVERNS
Douglas—121 Monroe St.

SHEFFIELD

HOTELS
McClain—19th St.

TUSCALOOSO

TOURISTS HOMES
M. A. Barnes—419 30th Ave.
G. W. Clopton—1516 25th Ave.

ARKANSAS

ARKADELPHIA

HOTELS
Hill's—1601 W. Piine St.
TOURIST HOMES
Mrs. B. Dedman—W. Caddo St.
Mrs. L. Cooper—W. Pine St.

RESTAURANTS
Richie Square Deal—Caddo St.
Hill's—River St.
BARBER SHOPS
Scott's—6th & Clay St.
Richie's Upright—16th St.

BRINKLEY

TOURIST HOMES
Davis—709 S. Main St.

EL DORADO

HOTELS
Brewster—E. & B. Sts.
Green's—303 Hill St.
TOURIST HOMES
C. W. Moore—5th & Lincoln Ave.
Dr. Dunning—7th & Columbia Ave.
BARBER SHOPS
Leaders—301 1/2 Hill St.
GARAGES
Williams—1305 E. 1st St.

FAYETTEVILLE

HOTELS
Mebbs—9 N. Willow St.
TOURIST HOMES
Mrs. S. Manuel—313 Olive St.
N. Smith—259 E. Center St.

FORT SMITH

HOTELS
M. Stratford—803 No. 9th St.
Ullery Inn—719 N. 9th St.
TOURIST HOMES
E. O. Trent—1301 N. 9th St.

HOPE

HOTELS
Lewis-Wilson

HOT SPRINGS

HOTELS
Crittenden—314 Cottage St.
The Reed House—115 Cottage St.
Crussader—501 Malvern Ave.
Poro Flat—410 Cottage Ave.
TOURIST HOMES
Barabin Villa—717 Pleasant St.
J. W. Rife—347 1/2 Malvern Ave.
Mrs. N. Fletcher—416 Pleasant Ave.
Mrs. C. C. Wilson—232 Garden St.
Mrs. H. Stilson—735 Pleasant St.
E. E. Lawson—706 Pleasant St.
Edmondson's—243 Ash Street
SANITARIUMS
Pyschean Baths—415 1/2 Malvern Ave.

LITTLE ROCK

HOTELS
The Marquette—522 W. 9th St.
Graysonia—809 Gaines St.
New Vincent—522½ West 9th St.
Tuckers—700½ W. 9th St.
C & C—522½ W. 9th St.

TOURIST HOMES
Mrs. T. Thomas—1901 High St.
Lafayette—904 State Street

RESTAURANTS
Lafayette—904 State St.
College—16th & Bishop
Johnson's—610 W. 9th St.
DeLuxe—203 E. Washington
DeLuxe—724 W. 9th St.
Dean's—904 State Street
Brown Bomber—W. 9th Street

BEAUTY PARLORS
Myrtles—1822 High St.
Woods—16th & High St.
Sue's—919 W. 9th St.
Lafayette—914 State Street

BEAUTY CULTURE SCHOOLS
Velvatex—1004 State Street
Velvia—814 Chester Ave.

TAVERNS
Ferguson's—14th & High Street

NIGHT CLUBS
Shangri-La—904 State Street
Lafayette—9th & State Street

BARBER SHOPS
Whitney—524 W. 9th St.
East End—1005½ Apperson
Century—609 W. 9th St.
Elite—622 W. 9th St.
Fontaine's—710 W. 9th St.
Century—610 West 9th Street
Woods—1523—High Street

LIQUOR STORES
Ritz—1511 Wright Ave.
Jones—528 W. 9th St.

SERVICE STATIONS
Lee's—1401 High St.
Spoon's—14th & High St.
Anderson—8th & State St.

GARAGES
Fosters—1400 W. 10th St.
Lee's—9th & Chester Street

In Our Next Edition
Make it a Point to Have Your Name Inserted Under the Proper Classification

DRUG STORES
Floyd—602 W. 9th St.
Children's—9th & Gaines

TAILORS
Miller—916 Gaines St.
Crenshaw—709 W. 9th St.
Dunn—2719 E. 2nd St.
Metropolitan—618 W. 10th St.
B & F—1005 Apperson St.

North LITTLE ROCK

HOTELS
Oasis—1311 E. 3rd St.

TOURIST HOMES
De Lux Court—2720 E. Broadway

RESTAURANTS
Jim's—908 Cedar St. N. L. R.
Nore Vean's—1101 E. 6th St.
Ceats—Henry—No. 67

ROAD HOUSE
Oasis—1311 East 3rd Street

BARBER SHOPS
College—1523 High St.

CAMDEN

TOURIST HOMES
Mrs. Benj. Williams—N. Main Street
Mrs. Hugh Hill—S. Main Street

RESTAURANT
Jim Summers—717 S. Main Street

BEAUTY SHOPS
Glady's—219 E. Washington St.

BARBER SHOPS
Lincoln—215 E. Washington St.

TAVERNS
Patton's—212 Short St.
Daniel's—North Adams St.
Jones—309 Monroe St.

LIQUOR STORES
Package—715½ Main St.
Summers—715½ S. Main Street

GARAGE
Mollette—N. Main Street

SOUTH CAMDEN
ROAD HOUSE
Henry Hanson—Cross Street

PINE BLUFF

HOTELS
P. K.—3rd & Alabama Sts.
Marietta—3rd & Louisiana Sts.
Smith's—East Third St.
Pee Kay—300 E. 3rd Street

TOURIST HOMES
Mrs. K. L. Bell—1111 W. 2nd Ave.
M. J. Hollis—1108 W. 2nd Ave.

RESTAURANTS
Shelton's—200 E. 3rd Street
Duck Inn—405 N. Cedar Street

BARBER SHOP
Nappy Chin—217 State Street

BEAUTY PARLOR
Pruitt's—1317 W. Baraque Street
BEAUTY SCHOOLS
DeLuxe—221 E. 3rd St.
Jefferson—1818 W. 6th Ave.
SERVICE STATION
Anderson—100 S. Mulberry St.
GARAGE
Alley's—1101 N. Cedar Street

FORDYSE
RESTAURANTS
Harlem—211 1st St.

HELENA
SERVICE STATIONS
Stark's—Rightor & Walnut Sts.

RUSSELLVILLE
TOURIST HOMES
Mrs. M. Jackson—Herman St.
E. Latimore—318 S. Huston Ave.

TEXARKANA
HOTELS
Brown's—312 W. Elm St.
TOURIST HOMES
G. C. Mackey—102 E. 9th St.
RESTAURANTS
Grant's Cafe—830 Laurel St.
BEAUTY PARLORS
M. B. Randall—1105 Laurel St.
BARBER SHOPS
G. Powell—106 E. 9th St.
Williams—121 E. 9th St.
SERVICE STATIONS
Smith & Rand—723 W. 7th St.

ARIZONA

DOUGLAS
TOURIST HOMES
Faustina Wilson—1002-16th St.
RESTAURANTS
Blue Bird Inn—361-9th St.

NOGALES
RESTAURANTS
Bell's Cafe—325 Morley Ave.

PHOENIX
HOTELS
Winston Inn—1342 E. Jefferson St.
Rice's—535 E. Jefferson St.
TOURIST HOMES
Mrs. L. Stewart—1134 E. Jefferson
Gardener's—1229 E. Washington St.
RESTAURANTS
Alhambia—1246-48 E. Wash. St.
Town Talk—1202 E. Jefferson Street
H & H—537 E. Jefferson Street
Walker's—1303 E. Jefferson Street
BEAUTY PARLORS
Thelma's—533 E. Jefferson St.
Copelands—1316 E. Jefferson St.
M. Parker—547 E. Jefferson St.
C. Jackson—1238 E. Madison St.

BARBER SHOPS
Hagler's—111 So. 2nd Street
Bryant's—620 S. 7th Ave.
TAVERNS
Vaughn's—1248 E. Washington Ave.
May's—1645 E. Madison Street
NIGHT CLUBS
Elks—7th Avenue & Tonto
SERVICE STATION
Super—13th & Washington Street
GARAGES
Tourist—126 S. 1st St.
Burly Ridue—126 So. 1st Street
DRUG STORES
R. D. Davis—1127 W. Buckeye Rd.
Johnson's—1140 E. Washington Street

TUSCON
TOURIST HOMES
Criterion Rooms—138 W. Ochoa St.
RESTAURANTS
Hill's Cafe—354 S. Meyer St.

YUMA
HOTELS
Brown's—196 N. Main St.

CALIFORNIA

BERKLEY
BEAUTY PARLORS
Little Gem—1511 Russell St.
BARBER SHOPS
Success—2946 Sacramento St.
TAVERNS
Schaeffer's—2940 Sacramento St.

EL CENTRO
HOTELS
The Roland—201 E. Main St.
TOURIST HOMES
Mrs. L. Augustas—420 Commercial Ave.
RESTAURANTS
Pearl McKinney Lunch—301 Main St.

FRESNO
HOTELS
Claren—145 N. Front Street
TOURIST HOMES
La Silve—841 F St.
RESTAURANTS
Taylor's—1402 C St.
Collins—847 'G' St.
DeLuxe—1228 'F' St.
Stella's—1861 'G' St.
Stella's—1861-G. Street
New Jerico—101 Church Street
BEAUTY PARLORS
Rosebud—835 G. Street
Clara's—855 'G' St.
Ruth's—1816 F. Street
Clara's—855 G. Street
Golden West—1032 - F. Street

BARBER SHOPS
  DeLuxe—725 'G' St.
  Golden West—1032—'F' St.
  Magnolia—602 F. Street
  Sportman's—855 G. Street
  Esquire—1011 G. Street
TAVERNS
  20th Century—1401 - F. Street
GARAGE
  Buddy Lang's—1335 - F. Street
  Frank's—1326 Fresno Street
TRAILER PARKS & CAMPS
  Barnes Drive In—1412 "F" St.
TAILORS
  Jackson's—1205 Sacramento Street

LOS ANGELES

HOTELS
  Clark—1824 Central Ave.
  Arcade—542 Ceres Avenue
  Lincoln—549 Ceres Ave.
  Sheridan—1824 Central Avenue
  McAlpin—648 Stanford Ave.
  Elite—1217 Central Avenue
  Olympic—843 S. Central Avenue
  Regal—815 E. 6th St.
  Sojourner's—1119 E. Adams Blvd.
  Kentucky—1123 Central Ave.
  Avon—405 S. Hewitt
  Dunbar—4225 S. Central Ave.
  Morris—809 E. 5th Street
  Glacier—523 Stanford Street
TOURIST HOMES
  Mrs. B. Hoffman—760 W. 17th St.
RESTAURANTS
  Marble Inn—1820 Imperial H'way
  Robertson's—4815 S. Central Avenue
  Chief—4400 S. Avalon Blvd.
  Ivie's—1105½ E. Vernon Avenue
  Pig N' Pat—4200 S. Central Avenue
  Henry Bros.—10359 Wilmington (WATTS)
  Banks—4019 S. Avalon Blvd.
  Nita's—125 W. Vernon Avenue
  John's—3519 S. Western
  Woodson's—Jefferson & Raymond Sts.
  Eddie's—4201 S. Central Avenue
  Blue Room—9900 S. Central Avenue
  Casa Blanca—2801 S. San Pedro St.
  Gingham—111 N. San Pedro Avenue
  Zombie—5432 S. Central Avenue
  Bobbie's—4001 Avalon Avenue
  The Fawn—Western & 29th St.
  Arc—4067 S. Central Avenue
  Shadowland—4505 Avalon Avenue
  Hi Jenks—4428 Avalon Avenue
  Waffle Shop—1063 E. 43 Street
  Clifton's—618 S. Olive Street
  Digby—1st & Alameda Street
BEAUTY PARLORS
  Creole—2221 Central Ave.
  Mary Esther—1709 E. 103rd St.
  Tex—2830 S. San Pedro St.
  Sherwoods—5113 S. Central Avenue
  Studio—2515 S. Central
  Continental—5203 Hopper Avenue
  Anna Mae's—4436 Avalon Avenue

Gorum—5440 S. Central Avenue
Louise—816 E. 5th St.
Triangle—43 San Pedro & Walls Sts.
Colonial—1813½ S. Central Avenue
Dunbar—4225 S. Central Avenue
M. Wilson—2818 S. Central Avenue
Beauty Salon—1195 East 35th Street
BARBER SHOPS
  Hotel—1808 S. Central Ave.
  Elite—4204 S. Central Avenue
  Connie's—2204 S. Central Avenue
  Bertha's—1434 W. Jefferson Boulevard
  Personality—4222 S. Central Ave.
  Williams—3615 S. Western
  Echo—43rd & Central Ave.
TAVERNS
  Marble Inn—1820 Imperial Highway
  Margot—5259 S. Central Avenue
  Emeral Room—901 E. 6th St.
  Emerald Room—901 E. 6th St.
  Golden Gate—1719 E. 103rd St.
  Paradise—5505 S. Central Avenue
  Samba—5th & Towns Avenue
  Onyx—1808 S. Central Avenue
  Crisbar—2829 S. Western Avenue
  Reney's—2023 S. Central Avenue
  Johnson's—4201 S. Main Street
  Casa Blanca—2801 S. San Pedro.
NIGHT CLUBS
  Club Alabam—4215 S. Central Avenue
  Down Beat—4201 S. Central Avenue
  Plantation—108th & Central
  Cafe Society—2711 S. San Pedro Avenue
  Basket Room—3219 S. Central Avenue
  Harlem—118th & Parmalee Sts.
  Rumboogie—1751½ E. 103rd St. (WATTS)
  Harlem—11812 Parmalee
  Tommy Brookins—1808 S. Central Ave.
  Billy Bergs—1354 N. Vine Street
ROAD HOUSE
  Casa Blanca—2801 S. San Pedro St.
LIQUOR STORES
  House of Morgan—2729 S. Central
  Mike's—10959 Wilmington (WATTS)
  Dunbar—4223 S. Central Avenue
  Jackson's—5501 S. Central Avenue
SERVICE STATIONS
  Valentine's Service—2657 S. Western Ave.
  Newton's—3903 S. Central Avenue
  Hopkins Signal Ser.—3426 Central Ave.
  Long's—2732 S. Central Ave.
  Carner's—4500 S. Avalon Avenue
  Simpkins & Cower—2227 S. Central Ave.
  Si Johnson's—3500 S. Western Ave.
  Tom's—1424 W. Jefferson Blvd.
  Hughes—2901 W. Jefferson Blvd.
  Brock—1246 W. Jefferson Blvd.
  R. A. & S.—Jefferson & Griffith
  Garcia—52nd Pl. and Central
GARAGES
  Parkers—2100 E. 103rd St.
  La Clare—Jefferson at Hill
  McAdam's—1448 W. Jefferson Blvd.
  Bill's—4106 Avalon Blvd.
  Alexander's—Jefferson & Griffith

AUTOMOTIVE
Lee's—4820 S .Central Avenue
Auto Parts—864 N. Virgil Avenue

DRUG STORES
Allums—4375 S. Central Avenue
Doctor's—4012 S. Central Avenue
Medical—3112 S. Western Avenue
Martinas—4406 Avalon Avenue
Slopers—2100—W. Jefferson Blvd.

TAILORS
Bader's—1840 E. 103rd St.
Delta—8512 Compton Avenue
Duver Bros.—811 E. 5th St.
Progressive—4302 S. Central Avenue
Beason—2901 S. Western Ave.

ELSINORE

MOTEL
Geo. Moore—407 Scrivener Street

HOLLYWOOD

TOURIST HOME
Jam. W. Brown—2881 Seattle Dr.

OAKLAND

HOTELS
Warren—1252 7th St.
TOURIST HOMES
Mrs. A. C. Clark—805 Linden St.
Mrs. H. Williams—3521 Grove St.
RESTAURANTS
The Villa—1724 7th St.
BEAUTY PARLORS
Personality—3613 San Dablo Avenue
TAVERNS
Overland Cafe—1719 7th St.
Rythm Buffet—1704 7th St.
SERVICE STATIONS
Summers—1251-7th St.
McCabe—5901 Adeline St.
Signal—800 Center St.
GARAGES
Bufford's—5901 Aldine St.

PASADENA

RESTAURANTS
Hub—Orange Grove at Fair Oaks
TAVERNS
Kentucky—1067 N. Fair Oaks
SERVICE STATIONS
Penn. Mobile—1096 Lincoln Ave.
Stacy's—920 N. Fair Oaks Avenue

SAN BERNADINO

TOURIST HOMES
S. M. Carlton—939 W. 6th St.

SAN DIEGO

HOTELS
Douglass—206 Market St.
Simmons—542 6th Avenue
Y. W. C. A.—2905 Clay St.
Y. M. C. A.—2905 Clay St.

TOURIST HOMES
Johnson's—18 N. 30th St.
RESTAURANTS
Sun—421 Market Street
Brown Hostess—2816 Imperial Ave.
SERVICE STATION
Weber's—2nd & Market Street
Woodson's—30th & K Streets
TAVERNS
Night Hawk—2971 Market Street
TAILORS
Clever—2606 Imperial Avenue
Imperial—2751 Imperial Avenue
DRUG STORES
Imperial—30th & Imperial Avenue

SAN FRANCISCO

HOTELS
Buford—1969 Sutter St.
The Scaggs—1715 Webster St.
Powell—Powell & Market Sts.
TOURIST HOMES
Mrs. F. Johnson—1788 Sutter St.
Helen's Guest House—1951 Sutter St.
RESTAURANTS
Calif. Theatre—1605 Post Street
BEAUTY PARLORS
Arineica's—1928 Fillmore St.
TAVERNS
Jack's—1931 Sutter St.
NIGHT CLUBS
Town Club—1963 Sutter St.
DRUG STORES
Riggan's—2600 Sutter St.

SANTA MONICA

TAVERNS
La Nobita—1807 Belmont Place

TULARE

TOURIST HOMES
South "K" St.—330 South "K" St.
TAVERNS
King's—322-24 South K. St.

VALLEJO

TAVERNS
Cotton Club—Virginia & Branciforte

VICTORVILLE

TOURIST HOMES
Murray's Dude Ranch

COLORADO

COLORADO SPRINGS

TOURIST HOMES
G. Roberts—418 E. Cucharras St.
L. C. Alford—509 N. Boyer St.

DENVER

HOTEL
Hildreth—2152 Arapahoe Street

TOURIST HOMES
Mrs. G. Anderson—2119 Marion St.
Mrs. W. Graham—2544 Emerson St.
R. B. Anderson—2421 Ogden St.
Mrs. A. S. Fisher—2355 High St.

RESTAURANTS
King's—2359 Marion St.
Red Booster—2622 Welton St.
Sugar Bowl—2832 Welton St.
Mac's—2635 Welton St.
Royal—2536 Washington St.
Mary's—714 E. 26th Avenue
A & A—2359 Marion St.
Warners—1857 Champa St.
St. Louis—2856 Welton St.
Green Lantern—2859 Fremont
Da-Nite—1430 22nd Avenue
B & E—2847 Gilpin St.
Dew Drop Inn—2715 Welton St.
Nu Way—1025 21st St.
Sugar Bowl—2832 Welton Street
Two Friends—1857 Champa Street
Down Beat—609 - 27 Street

BEAUTY PARLORS
Landers 2460 Marion St.
Unique—2547 Welton St.

Ford—2527 Humboldt St.
Myrtle's—2404 Clarkson St.
BARBER SHOPS
Dunbar—2741 Welton St.
Roxy—2559 Welton St.
20th Century—2727 Welton St.
W. A. Stephens—2650 Welton St.
TAVERNS
Rossonian Lounge—2650 Welton Street
Andersons—715 E. 26th Avenue
Arcade—739 E. 26th Avenue
Archie's—2449 Larimer St.

LIQUOR STORES
Lincoln—2636 Welton St.
18th Ave.—1108 E. 18th Avenue
Aristocrat—3101 William St.

SERVICE STATIONS
Mac's—2637 Welton St.
Da-Nite—728 E. 26th Avenue
White—2655 Downing St.
Plazer—E. 22nd & Humboldt Sts.

GARAGES
Mattherson's—2637 Welton St.
Mac's—2637 Welton Street

TAXI CABS
Ritz—2721 Welton St.

DRUG STORES
Rocy Mt.—23rd and Champa Sts.
T. K.—27th and Larimer Sts.
Ideal—28th & Downing
V. H. Meyers—22nd & Downing Sts.
Atlas—2701 Welton St.

TAILORS
Arcade—739 E. 26th St.
White House—2863 Welton St.
B & B—1710 E. 25th Avenue
Ace—2220 Downing St.

GREENLEY

TOURIST HOMES
Mrs. E. Alexander—106 E. 12th St.

LA JUNTA

TOURIST HOMES
Mrs. R. Mitchell—322 W. 1st St.
Mrs. Moore—301 Lewis Avenue
Mrs. H. Tittsworth—325 Maple Avenue

PUEBLO

HOTELS
Perry—231 S. Victoria St.

TOURIST HOMES
Mrs. T. Protho—918 E. Evans Avenue
C. Forehand—1003 Spruce St.

TRINIDAD

TOURIST HOMES
Mrs. C. Brooks—114 W. 3rd St.

CONNECTICUT

BRIDGEPORT

HOTELS
Y. W. C. A.—237 John St.
TOURIST HOMES
Mrs. M. Barrett—83 Summer St.
Mrs. E. Lawrence—68 Fulton St.
GARAGES
W & T—179 William St.

HARTFORD

HOTELS
Parrish Rooming House—26 Walnut St.
TOURIST HOMES
Mrs. Johnson—2016 Main St.
BEAUTY SHOPS
Quaility—1762 Main St.
BARBER SHOPS
Williams—1978 Main Street
TAVERNS
Turf Club—2243 Main St.

NEW HAVEN

HOTELS
Phyllis Wheatley—108 Canal St.
Hotel Portsmouth—91 Webster Avenue
TOURIST HOMES
Dr. M. F. Allen—65 Dixwell Avenue
Mrs. S. Robinson—54 Dixwell Avenue
Mrs. C. Raone—68 Dixwell Avenue
RESTAURANTS
Mrs. Griggs—146 Dixwell Avenue
Ruth's—222 Dixwell Avenue
Montrey—265 Dixwell Avenue
BEAUTY PARLORS
Mme. Ruby—175 Goffe St.
Harris—138 Goffe St.
Glady's—624 Orchard Street
Ethel's—152 Dixwell Avenue
SCHOOL OF BEAUTY CULTURE
Modern—170 Goffe St.

NEW LONDON

TOURIST HOMES
Home of the Bachelor—20 Brewer St.
Hempstead Cottage— 73 Hempstead St.
Mrs. E. Whittle—785 Bank St.
BEAUTY PARLOR
Boone's—96 Main Street

STAMFORD

HOTELS
GLADSTONE—Gay St.
TOURIST HOMES
Robert Graham—37 Hanrahan Ave.
NIGHT CLUBS
Sizone—136 W. Main St.

WATERBURY

HOTELS
Jones—64 Bishop St.
TOURIST HOMES
Mrs. A. Dunham—208 Bridge St.
Community House—34 Hopkins St.

WEST HAVEN

TAVERNS
Hoot Owl—374 Beach St.

DELAWARE
DOVER

HOTELS
Cannon's—Kirkwood St.
Cannon's—Division St.
Caleb Brown—Lincoln St.
Dean's—Forrest St.
Mosely's—Division St.
Moseley's—Division St.
Weston's—Division St.

TOWNSEND

HOTELS
Rodney—Dupont Highway-Rt. 13

WILMINGTON

HOTELS
Royal—703 French St.
Anderson—716 French St.
Y. M. C. A.—10th Ave. and Walnut St.
Y. W. C. A.—10th Ave. and Walnut St.
TOURIST HOMES
Miss W. A. Brown—1306 Tatnall St.
Mrs. E. Till—1008 French St.
RESTAURANTS
Christian Assn. Bldg.—10th & Walnut St.
BEAUTY PARLORS
Mrs. M. Anderson—916 French St.
BARBER SHOPS
Burton's—8th and Walnut St.
NIGHT CLUB
Spot—7th and 8th on French St.
SERVICE STATIONS
Esso—8th and 9th on King

DISTRICT OF COLUMBIA
WASHINGTON

HOTELS

JOHNSON'S HOTEL ————

1502 - 13TH ST., N. W.

ALL OUTSIDE ROOMS

HOT & COLD WATER IN EVERY ROOM

Joseph M. Johnson. Prop. Phone No. 6510

Henry—1825 13th St. N. W.
Mid-City—7th & 'N' Sts. N. W.

JOHNSON'S Jr. HOTEL ————

1509 VERMONT AVE., N. W.

HOT & COLD WATER IN EVERY ROOM
ALL OUTSIDE ROOMS

JOSEPH R. JOHNSON, PROP.

HOTELS
Whitelaw—13th & 'T' Sts. N. W.
J. Y's—16th & 'G' Sts. N. W.
Dunbar—U St. & 15th St., N. W.
Y. M. C. A.—1816 12th St. N. W.
Y. W. C. A.—901 Rhode Is. Ave. N. W.

TOURIST HOMES
Mrs. L. Fowler—1449 'Q' St. N. W.
Mrs. R. Lee—1212 Girad St. N. W.
Towles—1342 Vermont Ave., N. W.
Bailey's—2533 - 13th St., N. W.
Modern—3006 - 13th St., N. W.

TAVERNS
Holleywood—1940 9th St. N. W.
Liberty—910 5th St. N. W.
Harrison's Cafe—455 Florida Ave. N. W.
Service Grill—12th & 'V' Sts. N. W.
Off Beat—1849 - 7th St., N. W.
Kenyon—Ga. Avenue & Kenyon St., N. W.
Brentwood—4526 Rhode Island Ave., N. E.
Capitol—1224 U St., N. W.
Chuck's 1334 V St., N. W.
Club Liberty—910 - 5th St., N. W.

RESTAURANTS
Keys—7th & 'T' St. N. W.
Clore—7th & 'T' Sts. N. W.
Chicken Paradise—1210 U. St., N. W.
Earl's—1218 U St., N. W.
Sugar Bowl—2830 Georgia Ave., N. W.
Pig N Pit—1214 - 14th St., N. W.
Shrimp Hut—807 Florida Avenue, N. W.
Casbah—1211 U St., N. W.
Uptown—807 Florida, N. W.
Johnson's—1909 - 14th St., N. W.
Mother Froman's—1108 9th St., N. W.
The Hour—1937 - 11th St., N. W.
Jackson's—1831 Weltberger St., N. W.

LIQUOR STORES
Peoples—719 - 11th St., N. W.
S & W—1428 - 9th St., N. W.
Ney's—1013 Penna. Ave., N. W.
Shuster's—101 H St., N. W.
Masters—714 K St., N. W.

BARBER SHOPS
Florida—1803 Florida Ave., N. W.

BEAUTY PARLORS
Apex—1417 'U' St. N. W.
The Royal—1800 'T' St. N. W.
Elite—1806 Florida Ave., N. W.
Vanity Box—1515 - 9th St., N. W.
Lil's—1327 - 11th St., N. W.
Green's - 1825 - 18th St., N. W.
A. Marie—3114 - 11th St., N. W.
Bandbox—2036 - 18th St., N. W.

NIGHT CLUBS
Bali—1901 14th St. N. W.
Caverns—11th & 'U' St. N. W.
Republic Gardens—1355 'U' St. N. W.
Grand Terrace—3925 Benning Rd., N. E.
Club Bali—1901 - 14th St., N. W.
Club Caverns—11th & U St., N. W.

SERVICE STATIONS
Brown's—Georgia Ave. & 'V' St.
B. Barker—Florida Ave. & 8th St.
Engelberg—1783 Florida Ave., N. W.

GARAGES
University—Rear 1019 Columbia Rd. N. W.
TAILORS
W. R. Reynolds—1808 Florida Ave., N. W.

FLORIDA
DAYTONA BEACH
TOURIST HOMES
M. Littleton—522 S. Campbell St.
RESTAURANTS
Rotisserie—2nd & walnut St.
Casa Blanca 899 Cypress St.
C & B 566 Capbell St.
TAVERNS
Palms—walnut & 2nd Sts.
LIQUOR STORE
Hank's—610 S. Campbell St.
SERVICE STATIONS
Kirkland—Campbell & Orange Ave.

DELRAY BEACH
TAVERNS
Manfield—N. W. 1st St.

FORT LANDERDALE
HOTELS
Hill—430 N. W. 7th Ave.
TAVERNS
Windsor

JACKSONVILLE
HOTELS
Blue Chip—514 Broad St.
Richmond—422 Broad St.
TOURIST HOMES
Craddock—45th & Moncrief
Alpine Cottage—714 W. Ashley St.
E. H. Flipper—739 W. Church St.
L. D. Jefferson—1834 Moncrief Rd.
B. Robinson—128 Orange St.
G. L. Martin—702 W. Beaver St.
C. H. Simmons—434 W. Ashley St.
NIGHT CLUBS
Two Spot—45th & Moncrief Rd.

LAKE CITY
TOURIST HOMES
Ben-Flo—720 E. Leon St.

LAKELAND
TOURIST HOMES
Mrs. A. Davis—518 W. 1st St.
Mrs. J. Davis—842½ N. Florida Ave.
Mrs. J. Boyd—Missouri Ave.

LIBERIA
LIQUOR STORES
Blue Chip—2200 Simon Street

MIAMI
HOTELS
Mary Elizabeth—642 N. W. 2nd Ave.
Dorsey—941 N. W. 2nd Avenue

33

BEAUTY PARLORS
Progressive—1324 N. W. 1st Court
Williams—1214 N. W. 3rd Avenue
Elizabeth—175 N. W. 11th Terrace
Charlows—1730 N. W. 1st Court
Minnie's—1469½ N. W. 5th Avenue
BEAUTY SCHOOLS
Sunlight—1011 N. W. 2nd Avenue
BARBER SHOPS
Smith's—262 N. W. 17th St.
TAVERNS
Star—3rd Ave. & 15th St. N. W.
NIGHT CLUBS
Fiesta—627 N. W. 2nd Avenue
LIQUOR STORES
Cuban—1701 N. W. 4th Avenue
Ideal—175 N. W. 11th St.
Plantation—N. W. 14th St. & 3rd Ave.
Henry's—379 N. W. 14th St.
TAILORS
Valet—506 N. W. 14th St.
TAXI
Brown's—N. W. 8th St. & 2nd Ave.

ORLANDO
HOTELS
Wells Bilt—509 W. South St.

PENSACOLA
RESTAURANTS
Rhumboogie—509 E. Salamanca Street
TAILORS
Reese—307 E. Wright Street

SEBRING
RESTAURANTS
Brown's—406 Lemon St.

ST. AUGUSTINE
TOURIST HOMES
F. H. Kelley—83 Bridge St.
H. G. Tye Apts.—132 Central Avenue

TAMPA
HOTELS
Central—1028 Central Avenue
Dallas—829 Zack St.
DeLux—822 Constant St.
RESTAURANTS
Bruce's—813 Scott St.
TAVERNS
Little Savory—Central & Scott

WEST PALM BEACH
RESTAURANTS
Silver Bar Grill—615 8th St.

GEORGIA
ALBANY
TOURIST HOMES
Mrs. A. J. Ross—514 Mercer St.
Mrs. L. Davis—313 South St.
Mrs. C. Washington—228 S. Jackson St.

ATLANTA
HOTELS
Hotel Royal—214 Auburn Ave., N. E.
Mack—548 Bedford Place, N. E.
Savoy—239 Auburn A. (formerly Roosevelt)
Shaw—245 Auburn Ave.
James—241 Auburn Ave. N. E.
McKay—Auburn Ave.
Y. M. C. A.—22 Butler St.
TOURIST HOMES
Mrs. Connally-125 Walnut St. N. W.
RESTAURANTS
Suttons—312 Auburn Ave. N. E.
Dew Drop Inn—11 Ashby St. N. E.
Smitty's—Auburn Ave. N. E.
Hawk's306 Auburn
TAVERNS
Yeah Man—256 Auburn Ave. N. E.
Sportmans Smoke Shop—242Auburn N. E.
Butler's—1868 Simpson Road
BEAUTY PARLORS
Poro—250½ Auburn Avenue
BARBER SHOPS
Artistic—55 Decatur
Gate City—240 Auburn Ave., N. W.
NIGHT CLUBS
The Top Hat—Auburn Ave. N. E.
Poenciana—143 Auburn Avenue
SERVICE STATIONS
Harden's—848 Hunter Ave. Cor. Belle
Hall's 215 Auburn Ave., N. E.
GARAGES
South Side—539 Fraser St., N. E.

AUGUSTA
HOTELS
Crimm's—725 9th St.
Harlem—1145 9th St.
TOURIST HOMES
Mrs. M. Beaseley—1412 Twigg St.
WINE & LIQUOR STORES
Bollinger's—1114 Gwennett St.

BRUNSWICK
TOURIST HOMES
The Palms—1309 Glouster St.

COLUMBUS
HOTELS
Lowes—724 5th Ave.
Y. M. C. A.—521 9th St.
RESTAURANTS
Economy Cafe—519 8th St.
BEAUTY PARLORS
Ann's—832 4th Ave.
BARBER SHOPS
Sherrell's—First Avenue
NIGHT CLUB
Golden Rest—1026 7th Ave.
GARAGES
Seventh Avenue—816 7th Ave.

DUBLIN

TOURIST HOMES
Mrs. M. Burden—508 McCall St.
Mrs. R. Hunter—504 S. Jefferson
Mrs. M. Kea—405 S. Jefferson

EASTMAN

TOURIST HOMES
J. P. Cooper—211 College St.
Mrs. M. Mariano—408 1st Ave.

GREENSBORO

TOURIST HOMES
Mrs. C. Brown—Caanen Section
Mrs. E. Jeter—Railroad Section
Mrs. B. Walker—Springfield Section

MACON

HOTELS
Douglas—361 Broadway
Richmond—319 Broadway

TOURIST HOMES
Mrs. E. C. Moore—122 Spring St.
Brs. F. W. Henndon—139 1st Ave.

RESTAURANTS
Mables—Main Street
Red Front—417 Wall St.
Jean's—429 Cotton Avenue
West Side—222 Dempsey Avenue

BEAUTY PARLORS
Marquiata—554 New Street
La Bonita—455 Cotton Avenue
Carrie's—133 Forest Avenue
Lula Life—425 E. 2nd Street

TAILORS
Huschel—264 Broadway
Community—550 - 3rd Avenue

SERVICE STATION
Anderson's—Pursley at Pond Street

SAVANNAH

RESTAURANTS
Dreamland—43rd & Hopkins St.

BEAUTY PARLORS
Rudies'—1827 Ogeechee Road
Rose—348 Price St.

SCHOOL OF BEAUTY CULTURE
456 Montgomery St.

SERVICE STATIONS
Gibson's—442 West Broad Street

DRUG STORES
Moores'—37th & Florence

TAILORS
Halls—1014 W. Broad St.

TRAILERS PARK
Cocoanut Grove—Mrs. J. Cox

WAY CROSS

TOURIST HOMES
Mrs. K. G. Scarlett—843 Reynolds

ILLINOIS

CHICAGO

HOTELS
Ritz—409 E. Oakwood Blvd.
Alpha—2945 S. Michigan Blvd.
Como—5204 S. Parkway
Green Gables—3920 S. Lake Park Ave.
Du Sable—764 E. Oakwood Blvd.
Strode—820 E. Oakwood Blvd.
Almo—3800 Lake Park Ave.
Evans—733 E. 61st St.
Oakwood—820 E. Oakwood Blvd.
Perishing—6400 Cottage Grove Ave.
Praire—2836 Praire Ave.
S & S—4142 S. Park Ave.
Southway—6014 S. Parkway
Spencer—300 E. Garfield
Western—6357 Champlain Ave.
Grand—5044 S. Parkway
Tyson—4259 S. Parkway
Vincennes—601 E. 36th St.
Y. M. C. A.—3763 S. Wabash Ave.
Y. W. C. A.—4559 S. Parkway
Franklin—3942 Indianna Ave.
Lincoln—2901 State St.
Pompeii—20 E. 31st St.
New Hazie—3910 Indianna Ave.
Clarilge—51st & Michigan Ave.

TOURIST HOMES
Mabel Bank—712 E. 44th St.
Poro College—4415 S. Parkway

RESTAURANTS
Morris'—410 E. 47th St.
Wrights—3753 S. Wabash Ave.
A & J—105 E. 51st St.
Hurricane—345 E. Garfield Blvd.
Pitts—812 E. 39th St.
Palm Gardens—720 E. Oakwood Blvd.
400 Club—715 E. 63rd St.
Pioneer—533 E. 43rd St.
Pershing—755 East 64th Street

BEAUTY PARLORS
Matties'—4212 Cottage Grove Ave.

BARBER SHOPS
Bank's—209 E. 39th St.

TAVERNS
The palm—466 E. 47th St.
El Casino—823 E. 39th St.
Key Hole—3965 S. Parkway

NIGHT CLUBS
Boulevard Lounge—104 E. 51st St.
El Grotto—6400 Cottage Grove Ave.
Rhum-Boogie—353 E. Garfield Blvd.
820 Club—820 E. 39th St.
Show Boat—6109 S. Parkway

SERVICE STATIONS
Parkway—5036 S. Parkway
Waterford's—6000 S. Wabash Ave.
Standard—Garfield & S. Parkway
American Giants—5900 S. Wabash Ave.
Roosevelt—4600 S. Wabash Ave.

GARAGES
Grove—4751 S. Cottage Grove Ave.
Zephyr—4535 S. Cottage Grove Ave.
DRUG STORES
Partee—4308 S. Parkway
Thompson—545 E. 47th St.

CENTRALIA
TOURIST HOMES
Mrs. Claybourne—303 N. Pine St.
BEAUTY SHOPS
M. Coleman—503 N. Poplar St.
BARBER SHOPS
P. Coleman—503 N. Poplar St.
SERVICE STATIONS
Langenfield—120 N. Poular St.

DANVILLE
HOTELS
Just A Mere Hotel—218 E. North St.
TOURIST HOMES
Stewart—214 E. Main St.

EAST ST. LOUIS
TOURIST HOMES
P. B. Reeves—1803 Bond Ave.
W. E. Officer—2200 Missouri Ave.
NIGHT CLUBS
Cotton Club—1236 Mississippi Ave.

PEORIA
TOURIST HOMES
Clara Gibbons—923 Monson St.
RESTAURANTS
Twenty Grand—523 Smith St.
BEAUTY PARLORS
S. Thompson—809 Sanford Street
BARBER SHOP
Stone's—323 N. Adams St.
NIGHT CLUB
Bris Collins—405 N. Washington St.

SPRINGFIELD
HOTELS
Dudley—130 S. 11th St.
TOURIST HOMES
Mrs. M. Rollins—844 S. College St.
Mrs. B. Mosby—1614 E. Jackson St.
Mrs. H. Robbins—1616 E. Jackson St.
Mrs. G. Bell—625 N. 2nd St.
Mrs. E. Brooks—705 N. 2nd St.
Dr. Ware—1520 E. Washington St.

OTTAWA
TOURIST HOMES
Mrs. G. Danile—605 S. 3rd Ave.

ROCKFORD
HOTELS
Briggs—429 S. Court St.
TOURIST HOMES
Mrs. C.Gorum—301 Steward Ave.
Mrs. G. Wright—422 S. Court St.
S. Westbrook—515 N. Winnebago

WAUKEGAN
TOURIST HOMES
Mrs. R. Norwood—819 Mott Ave.

IDAHO
BOISE
TOURIST HOMES
Mrs. S. Love—1164 River St.

POCATEELLO
TOURIST HOMES
A. M. E. Parsnage—625 E. Fremont St.
Tourist Park—E. Fremont St.

INDIANA
ANDERSON
TAVERNS
Terrance Cafe—1411 Madison Ave.
RECREATION PARKS
Fox Lake Summer Resort 1½ miles S. W. of Angola

ELKHART
TOURIST HOMES
Miss E. Botts—336 St. Joe St.

EVANSVILLE
TOURIST HOMES
Mrs. B. Bell—672 Lincoln Ave.
Mrs. Lauderdale—309 Locust St.
Miss F. Snow—719 Oak St.
Community Ass'n—620 Cherry St.

FORT WAYNE
RESTAURANT
Leo Manuals'—1329 Lafayette St.

GARY
HOTELS
States'—1700 Washington St.

FRENCH LICK
HOTELS
Thurman—222 Indiana Ave.

INDIANAPOLIS
HOTELS
Y. M. C. A.—450 N. Senate Ave.
Y. W. C. A.—653 N. West St.
Anderson—Indianna Ave.
Ferguson—1102 N. Capitol Ave.
Marquis—1523 N. Capitol Avenue
HOTELS
Hawaii—406 Indiana Ave.
Zanzibar—420 N. Sinate Ave.
TOURIST HOMES
Morris Fur. Rms.—518 N. West St.

RESTAURANTS
Lasley's—510 Indiana Ave.
A. B.'s—413 Indiana Ave.
Broaden's—1645 N. Western Ave.
Parkview—321 N. California Ave.
Green's—709 Indiana Ave.
Stormy Weather—319 Indiana Ave.
Log Cabin—524 Indiana Ave.
CHINESE RESTAURANT
Yee Sen—545 Indiana
BEAUTY PARLORS
Petite—420 W. Michigan St.
Stephens & Childs—527 Indiana Ave.
Beauty Box—2704 Clifton St.
Dancy's—436 N. California Ave.
Smith's—446 Douglas St.
TAVERNS
Mayes Cafe—503 Indiana
Hambric Cafe—510 Indiana
Ritz—Sinate & Indiana
Sunset—875 Indiana
M. C.—544 W. Maryland St.
Blue Eagle—648 Indiana
Midway—736 Indiana
Panama—300 Indiana
SERVICE STATIONS
Harris—458 West 16th St.
GARAGES
25th St. Garage—553 W. 25th St.
DRUG STORES
Ethical—642 Indiana
TAILORS
Neighborhood—1642 Northwestern Ave.
Lee's—401 W. 29th St.

JEFFERSONVILLE

TOURIST HOMES
Charles Thomas—607 Missouri Ave.
Leonard Redd—711 Missouri Ave.

MARION

RESTAURANTS
Marshall's—414 E. 4th St.

KOKOMO

TOURIST HOMES
Mrs. C. W. Winburn—1015 Kennedy St.
Mrs. Charles Hardinson—812 Kennedy St.
Mrs. A. Woods—1107 N. Purdun St.
Mrs. S. D. Hughes—1045 N. Kennedy St.

LAFAYETTE

TAVERNS
Pekin Cafe—1702 Hartford St.

MICHIGAN CITY

TOURIST HOMES
Allen's—210 E.2nd St.

MUNCIE

HOTELS
Y. M. C. A.—905½ Willard St.

SOUTH BEND

RESTAURANTS
Smokes—432 S. Chapin St.

NEW ALBANY

TOURIST HOMES
J. D. Clay—513 Pearl St.

TERRE HAUTE

HOTELS
Booker—306 Cherry St.
TAVERNS
Dreamland Cafe—306 Cherry St.

WEST BADEN SPRINGS

HOTELS
Waddy

EVANSVILLE

TOURIST HOMES
Z. Knight—410 S. E. 9th St.

IOWA
CEDAR RAPIDS

TOURIST HOMES
Mrs. W. H. Lavelle—812 9th Ave. E.
Brown's—818 9th Ave. S. E.

DES MOINES

HOTELS
Y. W. C. A.—1407 Center St.
Parker-Roach—762½ 9th St.
La Marguerita—1425 Center Street
RESTAURANTS
Sampson—1246 E. 17th St.
Cunningham's—1602 E. University
Ida Bell's—783 11th St.
Watkins—833 Keo Way
Corinne's—1450 Walker Street
Bryson's—1115 Center Street
Gertrudes'—1308 Keo Way
Peck's—1180 - 13th Street
Community—1202 Center Street
Ida Bell's—783 Eleventh
Wilber & Mac's—1792 Walker Street
Buzz Inn—1000 Center Street
Herb's—1002 Center Street
Erma & Carrie's—1008 Center Street
William's—1200 East 16th St.
Welcome Inn—1545 Walker St.
BEAUTY PARLORS
Vo-Pon—1656 Walker St.
Berline—1206 Center St.
Polly's—1544 Walker St.
Evalon—762 W. 9th St.
Bernice's—911 W. 16th St.
Murlians—933 16th St.
Miniature—1143 Enis
Louie's—1204 Center Street
Ruth's—1049 4th Street

TAVERNS
  Herb's—1002 Center St.
SERVICE STATIONS
  Eagle—1955 Hubble Blvd.
  Mumford's—4th & Euclid Avenue
  Holgates—6th & Oak Park
  E & G Keo Way & Crocker
GARAGES
  4th Street—417 4th St.
  Hiland—705 - 6th Avenue
AUTOMOTIVES
  Andy's—E. University & Hubble
TAILORS
  National—808 - 12th Street
  Clean Craft—1300 - 6th Avenue
DRUG STORE
  Adams—E. 5th & Locust St.

DUBUQUE
TOURIST HOMES
  Mrs. P. Martin—712 University Ave.
  Mrs. Edwin Weaver—795 Roberts Ave.

OTTUMWA
TOURIST HOMES
  Mrs. J. Rose—802 N. Fellows
  William Bailey—526 Center Ave.
  J. H. Hewitt—512 Grant
  Harry Owens—814 W. Pershing

WATERLOO
TOURIST HOMES
  Mrs. B. F. Tredwell—928 Beach St.
  Mrs. Spencer—220 Summer St.
  Mrs. E. Lee—745 Vinton St.

KANSAS

ATCHISON
TOURIST HOMES
  Mrs. Geneva Miles—924 N. 9th St.
NIGHT CLUB
  Mrs. M. McDonald—10th & Spruce
DRUG STORES
  Henderson—7th & Division St.

BOGUE
TOURIST HOMES
  Tourist Court—Juntion Rt. U. S. 24

COFFEYVILLE
TOURIST HOMES
  Tourist Home—618 E. 5th St.

CONCORDIA
TOURIST HOMES
  Mrs. B. Johnson—102 E. 2nd St.
  Mrs. Glen McVey—328 East St.

EMPORIA
TOURIST HOMES
  Elliott's—816 Congress St.

EDWARDSVILLE
TOURIST HOMES
  Road House—Anderson's Highway 32 & Bitts Creek

FORT SCOTT
HOTELS
  Hall's—223½ E. Wall St.
TOURIST HOMES
  Peter Thomasun—114 S. Ransom St.

HIAWATHA
TOURIST HOMES
  Mrs. Mary Sanders—1014 Shawnee

HUTCHINSON
TOURIST HOMES
  Mrs. C. Lewis—400 W. Sherman

INDEPENDENCE
TOURIST HOMES
  Major McBee—418 S. 3rd St.

JUNCTION CITY
HOTELS
  Bridgeforth—311 E. 11th St.
TOURIST HOMES
  Mrs. B. Jones—229 E. 14th St .

LARNED
TOURIST HOMES
  Mrs. C. M. Madison—828 W. 12th St.
  Mrs. Mose Madison—518 W. 10th St.
  Mrs. John Caro—E. 16th St. & Johnson Av.

LAURENCE
HOTELS
  Snowden's—1933 Tennessee St.

LEAVENWORTH
TOURIST HOMES
  Mrs. J. Hamilton—720 N. 3rd St.
  Mrs. W. Shelton—216 Poplar St.

KANSAS CITY
RESTAURANT
  Keystone Club—4th & Freemen
  Duck Inn—5th & State Street
  Famous—12th & Forest
  Chat-Chew—1908 N. 5th Street
  Virgil's Place—1622 Gray Road
  M & T—2013 E. 12th Street
ROAD HOUSE
  De Moss—37th & Ben Balance Road
NIGHT CLUBS
  Flamingo—1916 N. 5th St.
  Congo—1932 - 5th St.
SERVICE STATION
  Dunn & McGee—7th & Garfield

GARAGE
Economy—1935 N. 5th St.
DRUG STORES
Whitney's—5th & Virginia
Cundiff—5th & Quindarf

MANHATTAN
TOURIST HOMES
Mrs. E. Dawson—1010 Yuma St.
Mrs. H. Jackson—830 Yuma St.

OTTAWA
TOURIST HOMES
Mrs. Folson—112 N. Poplar
Mrs. R. W. White—821 Cypress

PARSONS
TOURIST HOMES
Mrs. F. Williams—2216 Grand Ave.
Womack—2109 Morgan

TOPEKA
HOTELS
Dunbar—400 Vuincy St.
TOURIST HOMES
Mrs. E. Slaughter—1407 Monroe
TAVERNS
Macks'—400 Quincy St.
Power's Cafe—116 E. 4th St.

WICHITA
TOURIST HOMES
Oklahoma House—517½ N. Main St.
RESTAURANTS
Oklahoma Cafe—517 N. Main St.

KENTUCKY
ELIZABETHTOWN
TOURIST HOMES
A. Johnson—Valley Creek Road
Mrs. B. Tyler—Mile Stt.
M. E. Wintersmith—S. Dixie Ave.

HAZARD
TOURIST HOMES
Mrs. J. Razor—436 E. Main St.
Mrs. Jessie Richardson—

PADUCAH
TOURIST HOMES
Amy Cox—813 Washington St.

HOPKINSVILLE
TOURIST HOMES
Mrs. M. McGregor—200 E. First St.
L. McNary—113 Liberty St.
J. C. Hopkins—128 Liberty St.

LANCASTER
TOURIST HOMES
Burn's—Buford St.
Hord's—Buford St.
RESTAURANTS
Plum's—Buford St.
BARBER SHOPS
Hyatt's—Buford St.
BEAUTY PARLORS
Hilltop—Buford St.
GARAGES
Warren & Francis—N. Campbell St.

LINCOLN RIDGE
TOURIST HOMES
Lincoln Institute

LOUISVILLE
HOTELS
Allen—2516 W. Madison St.
Pythian Temple—10th & Chestnut
Walnut—615 Walnut St.
Y. W. C. A.—528 S. 6th St.
May's—623 S. 10th St.
TOURIST HOMES
Lee L. Brown—1014 W. Chestnut
Hattie Daniels—1512 W. Chestnut
RESTAURANTS
Eatmore—964 S. 12th St.
White Swann—1208 W. Walnut
Honey Dripper—1208 Breckinridge St.
Jones—525 S. 13th St.
Du Rez—Madison & 26th St.
Honey Dripper—1212 W. Breckenridge St.
Thompson's—419 So. 19th St.
Harry's—28th & Chestnut Sts.
W. & H.—432 S. 18th St.
California—1604 Gallagher St.
Club Hollywood—813 S. 6th St.
Jone's—525 S. 13th St.
West End—1929 W. Walnut St.
BEAUTY PARLORS
Scotty's—442 So. 21st St.
Bellonia—1625 Callagher St.
Mae Ella's—1110 W. Walnut St.
McKissick's—505 S. 8th St.
Scotty—422 S. 21st St.
Elizabeth's—962 S. 12th St.
Jones—409 S. 18th St.
Beauty Box—922 W. Walnut St.
Rose's—1813 W. Walnut St.
Willie's—639 S. 10th St.
BARBER SHOPS
Hunter's—1501 W. Chestnut St.
TAVERNS
Herman—1601 W. Walnut St.
Dave's—13th & Magazine
NIGHT CLUBS
Del Rey—Madison & 26th St.
LIQUOR STORES
Palace—12th & Walnut St.
Lyons—16th & Walnut St.
GARAGES
Eade's—2420 Cedar St.

TAXI CABS
Lincoln—705 W. Walnut
Dependable—1835 W. Walnut St.
Ave.—620 W. Walnut St.

LOUISIANA
BATON ROUGE
HOTELS
Ever-Ready 1325 Government St.
TOURIST HOMES
T. Harrison—1236 Louisiana Ave.
RESTAURANTS
Ideal Cafeteria—1501 E. Blvd.
TAVERNS
Waldo's—864 S. 13th St.
BEAUTY PARLORS
Carrie's—561 S. 13th St.
BARBER SHOPS
Malacher's—1310 Government St.
NIGHT CLUBS
Paradise—220 Boatnes St.
SERVICE STATIONS
Horatio's No. 1—1150 South St.
Horatio's No. 3—1607 Gov't. St.
ROAD HOUSES
Apex—Louise St.

BOGALUSA
TOURIST HOMES
Mrs. E. L. Raine—508 North Ave.

LAFAYETTE
TOURIST HOMES
Bourges—416 Washington St.
Mrs. A. Miles—302 Johns St.
J. Bondreaux—315 Stewart St.

LAKE CHARLES
TOURIST HOMES
Combre's Place—601 Boulevard

MANSFIELD
TOURIST HOMES
S. A. Wilson—N. Jefferson St.
W. Simpkins—Jenkins St.
BEAUTY SCHOOL
Annie Lou—615 Jenkins St.

MONROE
HOTELS
Turner's—1015 Desiard St.
TOURIST HOMES
R. H. Burns—700 Adams
L. B. Hortons—Congo St.

MORGAN CITY
TOURIST HOMES
Mrs. L. Williams— 719 Federal Ave.
Mrs. V. Williams—208 Union St.

NEW ORLEANS
HOTELS
Patterson—802½ S. Rampert St.
Vogue—2231 Thalia St.
North Side—1518 La Harpe St.
Gladstone—3435 Dryades St.
Astoria—225 S. Rampart St.
The Chicago—1310 Iberville St.
Paige—1038 Dryades Ave.
Riley—759 S. Rampart St.
Palace—1834 Annette St.
New Roxy—759 S. Rampart St.
Golden Leaf—1209 Saratoga St.
TOURIST HOMES
Mrs. F. Livaudais—1954 Jackson
N. J. Bailey—2426 Jackson Ave.
Mrs. King—2826 Louisiana Ave.
RESTAURANTS
Honey Dew Inn—115 Front St.
Club Crystal—1601 Dumaine
Place-of-Joy—2700 Melpomene St.
Pelican—S. Rampart at Gravier
Dooky—Cor. Orleans & Miro
Foster's Chicken Den—Cor. LaSalle &7th St.
92nd Club—2119 Orleans St.
The Gem—2601 Orleans St.
Hayes Chicken Shack—La. & Saratoga St.
Hide-away Inn—28 Desire St. & Rampart
Beck's—1520 N. Claiborne Ave.
Playhouse—2441 London Ave.
Portia's—2426 Louisiana Ave.
BARBER SHOPS
Lopez's—447 S. Rampart St.
BEAUTY PARLORS
Bessie's—1841 St. Ann St.
Thompson's—3429 Dryades St.
Ola's—1320 St. Bernard Ave.
SCHOOL OF BEAUTY CULTURE
Josephine's—1206 Pine
Poro—2217 Dryades St.
TAVERNS
Astoria—235 S. Rampart St.
Monte's—Jackson & S. Claiborne Ave.
Club Crystal—1601 Dumaine
Le Rendez-vous-7 Mille Post Gentilly H'way
Di Leo's—Ursuline & N. Robertson
NIGHT CLUBS
Dew Drop Inn—2836 La Salle St.
Shadowland—1921 Washington Ave.
Graystone—1900 Eagle St.
SERVICE STATIONS
Bill Board—2900 Claiborne Ave.
Ross—2620 S. Claiborne
Ross—1330 S. Broad St.
TAXICABS
Ed's—St. Bernard & N. Claiborne
Haney Dripper—Phone B—y3071
V-8 Cab Line—Felicity & Howard Sts.
Logan—2730 Felicity St.
DRUG STORES
Aprill—LaSalle & Washington
TAILORS
Martin's—1341 St. Anthony St.
Autocrat—1609 LaHarpe St.

Phone Jackson 9617　　　　　　　　　　　　　　On U. S. No. 90

E. L. Marsalis　　　　　　　　　　　　　　　　　J. L. Wicker

2900 S. Claiborne Ave.　　　　　　　　　　New Orleans, La.

    Repairs, Washing, Greasing, Tire—Battery Service & Complete
line of Standard Products.　　　　　　Tourist Information

E. L. Marsalis Sr. Prop.　　　　　　　　　Phone: CEDAR 4009

RIVERSIDE TOURIST COURT
3501 Riverside Drive - Jefferson Parish - New Orleans 20, La.
In Connection With - Bill Board Esso Service

41

TRAILER COURTS
Greenwood—Rt. 90—7½ miles P. T.

NEW IBERIA

TOURIST HOMES
M. Robertson—116 Hopkins St.
N. E. Cooper—913 Providence St.

OPELOUSAS

TOURIST HOMES
V. Arceneaux—723 E. Landry
H. Johnson—N. Market St.
B. Giron—S. Lombard St.

SCOTLAND
SERVICE STATIONS
Horatio's No. 2—Highway No. 61

SHREVEPORT

HOTELS
Hardy's—1726 Ford St.
Lloyd's—1229 Reynolds St.
RESTAURANTS
Wilson's—840 Williamson St.
Lighthouse Inn—2321 Milam St.
Saphronia's—815 Lawrence St.
Grand Terrace—Pierre & Looney St.
TOURIST HOMES
Grant Flats—1239 Reynolds
Mrs. J. Jones—1950 Hotchkiss
Mrs. A. Webb—1245 Reynolds
Mrs. W. Elder—1920 Hotchkiss
TAVERNS
A-Jack's—1836 Perrin St.
New Tuxedo—611 East 70th St.
Goldie's—238 Baker St.
SERVICE STATIONS
Ross'—901 Pierre St.
Pat's—Milan & Lawerence Sts.
William's-Milan & Ross-Milan & Pierre Ave.
TAILORS
3-Way—2415 Milan St.
Jones—1837 Looney St.
3 Way—2415 Milam St.

MAINE

AUGUSTA
TOURIST HOMES
Mrs. J. E. McLean—16 Drew St.

BANGOR
TOURIST HOMES
Mr. E. Dymond—339 Hancock Street

GARDNIER
TOURIST HOMES
Pond View—Pleasant Pond Road

OLD ORCHARD
TOURIST HOME
Mrs. Rose Cumming's—110 Portland Ave.

PORTLAND
HOTELS
The Thomas House—28 'A' St.

MARYLAND

ANNAPOLIS
HOTELS
Wright's—26 Calvert St.
NIGHT CLUBS
Washington—61 Washington St.

BALTIMORE
HOTELS
York—1200 Madison Ave.
New Albert—1224 Penna. Ave.
Smith's—Druid Hill Ave. & Paca St.
Majestic—1602 McCulloh St.
Y. W. C. A.—1916 Madison Ave.
Stokes—1500 Argylle Ave.
Y. M. C. A.—1600 Druid Hill Ave.
TOURIST HOMES
Mrs. E. Watsons—340 Blum St.
RESTAURANTS
Gorden's—1533 Druid Hill Ave.
Murry's—1423 Penn. Avenue
Spot Bar-B-Q—1530 Penna. Ave.
Club Barbeque—1519 Penna. Ave.
BEAUTY PARLORS
M. King—1510 Penna Ave.
Scott's—1526 Penna Ave.
Young's—613 W. Lafayette Ave.
La Blanche—1531 Penna. Ave.
BARBER SHOPS
Nottingham—1619 Penna A ve.
TAVERNS
Sugar Hill—2361 Druid Hill Ave.
Velma—Cor. Penn & Baker St.
Wagon Wheel—1638 Penna Ave.
The Alhambra—1520 Penna Ave.
Dreamland—1007 Penna Ave.
Gamby's—1504 Penna. Ave.
Frolic—1401 Penna. Ave.
NIGHT CLUBS
Little Comedy—1418 Penna
Ubangi—2213 Penna Ave.
Wonderland—2043-Penna
Casino—1517 Penna Ave.
20th Century—21 W. Oliver
LIQUOR STORES
D & D—890, Linden Ave.
Berman's—1439 Penna Ave.
Fine's—1817 Penna Ave.
Hackerman's—1733 Penna
TRAILER CAMP
Scott's—Eastern Ave. Rd., Box 593
SERVICE STATION
Esso-Presstman & Fremont
GARAGES
Jacks'—514 Wilson St.
Service—1415 Etting St.

BUENA VISTA

RESTAURANT
Eddie Bells—Defense Highway

COLTON

HOTELS
Shirley K
Conway's
Golden's

FREDERICK

TOURIST HOMES
Mrs. J. Makel—119 E. 5th St.
Mrs. W. W. Roberts—316 W. South
E. W. Grinage—22 W. All Saints
RESTAURANTS
Crescent—16 W. All Saint St.

HAGERSTOWN

TOURIST HOMES
Harmon—226 N. Jonat an St.

SALISBURY

TOURIST HOMES
M. L. Parker—110 Delaware Ave.

TURNERS CORNER

NIGHT CLUBS
Adam's

UPPER MARLBORO

TOURIST HOMES
Wm. Eaton—Leland Rd. & Cainds H'way

MASSACHUSETTS

ATTLEBORO

TOURIST HOMES
J. R. Brooks Jr.—54 James St.

BOSTON

HOTELS
Harriett Tubman—25 Holyoke St.
Mothers Lunch—510 Columbus Av.
Lucille—52 Rutland Sq.
TOURIST HOMES
Mrs. Williams—555 Columbus Ave.
Julia Walters-912 Tremont
Holeman—212 W. Springfield St.
M. Johnson—616 Columbus Ave.
Mrs. E. A. Taylor—192 W. Springfield St.
Guest House—193 Humbolt St.
RESTAURANTS
Western—431 Mass. Ave
Lonie Lee's—536 Columbus Ave.
Village—422 Mass. Ave.
Slades—958 Tremont St.
Estelle's—889 Tremont St.
Southern—505 Mass. Ave.
Oklahoma—975 Tremont Ave.
LaBid—708A Tremont St.
Charlie's—429 Columbus Ave.
Green Candle—395 Mass. Ave.

BEAUTY PARLORS
Clark-Merrill—505 Shawnut Ave.
Amy's—796 Tremont St.
Geneva's—808 Tremont St.
Estelle's—15 Greenwich Ave.
Mme. F. S. Blake—363 Mass. Ave.
E. L. Crosby—11 Greenwich Park
Mme. Enslow's—977 Tremont St.
W. Milliams—62 Hammond St.
Victory—46 W. Canton St.
E. West—609 Columbus Ave.
Ruth Evans—563 Columbus Ave.
Doris—795 Tremont St.
Rubinetta—961 Tremont St.
Beauty Box—781C Tremont St.
Lucile's—226 W. Springfield St.
Constance—414 Mass. Ave.
Atlas—716 Shawnut Ave.
Ester's—169A Springfield St.
Arizona—563 Columbus Ave.
Washington—985 Tremont
Lititia's—140 Linox St.
Jovennette's—109 Humbolt Ave.
Betty's—609 Columbus Ave.
BARBER SHOPS
Amity—1028 Tremont St.
Abbott's—974 Tremont St.
NIGHT CLUBS
Little Dixie—417 Mass. Ave.
Savoy—410 Mass. Ave.
SERVICE STATIONS
Maryland—690 Columbus Ave.
GARAGES
DePrest—255 Northampton
TAILORS
Garfield's—657 Shawaut Ave.
Savannah—612 Shawnut St.
Baltimore—1013 Tremont St.
Corry's—431 A Mass. Ave.
Chester's—189 W. Newton St.
Grady & Oliver—525 Shawnut St.

CAMBRIDGE

TOURIST HOMES
Mrs. S. P. Bennett—26 Mead St.

GREAT BARRINGTON

TOURIST HOMES
Mrs. I. Anderson—28 Rossiter St.

HYANIS

TOURIST HOMES
Zilphas Cottages—134 Oakneck Rd.

NORTH ADAMS

TOURIST HOMES
F. Adams—32 Washington Ave.

NEEDHAM

TOURIST HOMES
B. Chapman—799 Central Ave.

PITTSFIELD

TOURIST HOMES
M. E. Grant—53 King St.
Mrs. T. Dillard—109 Linden St.
Mrs. B. Jasper—66 Dewey Ave.
J. Marshall—124 Danforth Ave.

PLYMOUTH

TOURIST HOMES
Mrs. Taylor—11 Oak St.
W. A. Gray—47 Davis St.

RANDOLPH

RESTAURANTS
Mary Lee Chicken Shack—482 Main St.

ROXBURY

TOURIST HOMES
Mrs. S. Gale—168 Townsend St.
BEAUTY PARLORS
Ruth's—64 Humboldt St.
Charm Grove—90 Humboldt St.
Mme. Lovett—68 Humboldt St.
SERVICE STATIONS
Mac's—8 Coventry St.
Thompson's—1105 Tremont St.
TAILORS
Garfield's—657 Shawmut St.
Morgan's—355 Warren St.
Roxbury—52 Laurel St.
DRUG STORE
Douglas Square—1002 Tremont St.
Jaspan's—134 Harold St.

SOUTH HANSON

TOURIST HOMES
Modern—26 Reed St.
TRAILOR PARKS
Mrs. Mary B. Pina—26 Reed St.

STOCKBRIDGE

HOTELS
Park View House—Park St.

SPRINGFIELD

HOTELS
Springfield
BARBER SHOPS
Joiner's—97 Hancock Street
BEAUTY PARLORS
Law's—18 Hawley St.
TAILORS
American Cleaners—433 Eastern Ave.

SWAMPSCOTT

TOURIST HOMES
Mrs. M. Home—3 Boynton St.

WORCESTER

HOTELS
Worcester—Washington Square

RESTAURANTS
Dixie—143 Summer St.
Moffett's—47 Summer St.
BARBER SHOP
Buddy's—118 Summer St.
BEAUTY PARLORS
Bea's—8 Carwell St.
SERVICE STATION
Kozarian's—53 Summer St.
GARAGE
Bancroft—24 Portland St.
DRUG STORE
Bergwall—238 Main St.

WOBURN

TOURIST HOMES
Watts—10 High St.

MICHIGAN
ANN ARBOR

HOTELS
American—123 Washington St.
Allenel—126 El Huron St.
TOURIST HOMES
Mrs. E. M. Dickson—144 Hill St.

BATTLE CREEK

TOURIST HOMES
Mrs. F. Brown—76 Walters Ave.
Mrs. P. Grayson—22 Willow
Mrs. C. S. Walker—709 W. Van Buren

BALDWIN

SERVICE STATIONS
Bayak's—, Morgan, Prop.
Nolph's Super Service

BENTON HARBOR

NIGHT CLUBS
Research Pleasure Club—362 8th St.

BITELY

HOTELS
Kelsonia Inn—R. R. No. 1
Royal Breeze—On State Rt. 37

DETROIT

HOTELS
Touraine—4614 John R. St.
Gotham—111 Orchestra Place
Mark Twain—E. Garfield & Woodward
Biltmore—1926 St. Antoine St.
Tansey—2474 Antoine St.
Elizabeth—413 E. Elizabeth St.
Fox—715 Madison St.
Le Grande 1365 Lafayette St.
Norwood—550 E. Adams St.
Russell—615 E. Adams St.
Preyer—2476 St. Antoine St.
Crosstown—4652 Hastings St.

Touraine—4614 John R. St.
Terraine—John R. & Garfield
Northcross—2205 St. Antoine
Dewey—505 E. Adams St.
Davidson—556 E. Forest Ave.
Edenburgh—758 Westchester Ave.
Hotel - McGraw—5605 Junction
Old Rivers—2036 Hastings
Sportman's—3761 W. Warren Ave.

TOURIST HOME
Labland—39 Orchestra Place

RESTAURANTS
Blue Goose—4121 Hastings St.
Lunchonette—1949 Hastings St.
Pelican—4613 John R. St.
De Luxe—5423 Hastings
Jean's—6066 Brush
Vera's—John R & Palmer

BEAUTY PARLORS
Cleo's—4848 Hastings St.
Touraine—4626 John R. St.
Oakland—9313 Oakland Ave.
Powder Box—3737 Hastings St.
Elizabeth's—4848 Hastings St.
West Warren—4815 W. Warren Ave.

BARBER SHOPS
Swanson's—3415 Hastings St.
Bob's—4564 W. Warren Ave.

TAVERNS
Champion—Oakland & Holbrook
Horseshoe—606 Club
Bizerto—9006 Oakland Ave.
Owl—1540 Chene St.
Broad's—8825 Oakland

NIGHT CLUBS
666—666 E. Adams St.
Sportree's—2014 Hastings St.

ROAD HOUSES
Brown Bomber—421 E. Vernon H'way

SERVICE STATIONS
Murray's—1104 Holbrook St.
Johnson's—McGraw & 25th St.
Cobb's—Maple & Chene Sts.
Homer's—589 Madison Ave.

AUTOMOBILES
Davis Motor Co.—421 E. Vernon H'way

TAILORS
Kenilworth—131 Kenilworth
Blair—277 Gratist
Thomas—1024 Caniff Ave.
Hill's—8954 Oakland Ave.
Raglin—3636 W. Warren Ave.

DRUG STORES
Clay—Clay & Cameron Ave.
M. Dorsey—2201 St. Antoine St.
Kay—4766 McGraw Ave.
Barthwell's—Hastings & Benton

FLINT

TOURIST HOMES
T. Kelley—407 Wellington Ave.
T. L. Wheeler—1512 Liberty St.
Mrs. F. Taylor—1615 Clifford St.

GRAND JUNCTION

TOURIST HOME
Hamilton Farms—RFD No. 1

HARTFORD

TOURIST HOMES
Mrs. R. E. J. Wilson—210 E. 4th St.
Crosby's Farm

IDLEWILD

HOTELS
Eagles Nest

TOURIST HOMES
Edinburgh Cottage—Miss Herrone
B. Riddles
Meadow Lark Haven—Pine St.

RESTAURANTS
Lottie Roxborough—Box 837
Lorine Lunch—Baldwin Road

JACKSON

TOURIST HOMES
Mrs. W. Harrison—1215 Greenwood Ave.
Mrs. S. Collins—835 Adrian Ave.

LANSING

TOURIST HOMES
Mrs. M. Gray—1216 St. Joseph St.
M. Busher—1212 W. St. Joseph St.
Mrs. Lewis—816 S. Butler St.
Mrs. Cook—1220 W. St. Joseph St.
Mrs. Gaines—1406 Albert St.

MUSKEGON

TOURIST HOMES
R. C. Merrick—65 E. Muskegon Ave.
Rev. Fowler—937 McIllwraigh St.
R. A. Swift—472 W. Monroe

OSCODA

TOURIST HOMES
Jesse Colbath—Van Eten Lake

SHELBY TOWNSHIP

ROAD HOUSES
Joe Louis Farm—9700 Hamlin Road

SAGINAW

TOURIST HOMES
Mrs. E. Gant—312 S. Baum St.
Mrs. J. Curtley—439 N. Third St.
Mrs. P. Burnette—406 Emerson St.

SOUTH HAVEN

TOURIST HOME
Mrs. M. Johnson—Shady Nook Farm

WOODLAND

TOURIST HOME
Mrs. C. P. Tucker—Shangri - La

MINNESOTA

DULUTH

TOURIST HOMES
Jefferson—1119 W. Michigan Ave.

MINNEAPOLIS

HOTELS
Y. W. C. A.—809 N. Aldrich Ave.
Serville—246½ 4th Ave.
TOURIST HOMES
Phyllis Wheatley House—809 N. Aldrich Av.
RESTAURANTS
Bells Cafe—207 South 3rd St.

ST. PAUL

TOURIST HOMES
Villa Wilson—697 St. Anthony Ave.
RESTAURANTS
G. & G. Bar-B-Q—291 No. St. Albans

MISSISSIPPI

BILOXI

TOURIST HOMES
Mrs. L. Scott—421 Washington St.
Mrs. G. Bess—630 Main St.
A. Alcina—437 Washington St.

CLEVELAND

SERVICE STATIONS
7-11—Highway 61 at 8

COLUMBUS

HOTELS
Queen City—15th St. & 7th Ave.
TOURIST HOMES
M. J. Harrison—915 N. 14th St.
H. Sommerville—906 N. 14th St.
Mrs. L. Alexander—N. 12th St.
Mrs. I. Roberts—12th & 5th Ave. N.
Mrs. Chevis—1425 11th Ave. N.

GREENVILLE

TOURIST HOMES
Mrs. B. B. Clark—508 Obea St.
SERVICE STATION
Peoples—Nelson & Eddie St.

GRENADA

TOURIST HOMES
Mrs. K. D. Fisher—72 Adams St.
F. Williams—H'way 51 & Fairground Rd.
Henry's Lodge—H'way 51 & Fairground Rd.

HATTIESBURG

TOURIST HOMES
W. A. Godbolt—409 E. 7th St.
Mrs. A. Crosby—413 E. 6th St.
Mrs. S. Vann—636 Mobile St.

JACKSON

HOTELS
Wilson House—154 W. Oakley St.
TOURIST HOMES
Mrs. B. Marino—937 Grayson St.

RESTAURANTS
Shepherd's—604 North Farish St.
Home Dining Room—400 N. Farrish St.
BEAUTY PARLORS
Davis Salon—703 N. Farish
BARBER SHOPS
City—127 N. Farish
SERVICE STATIONS
Johnson's—536 N. Farish
GARAGES
Farish St.—748½ N. Farish

LAUREL

HOTELS
Bass—S. Pine St.
TOURIST HOMES
Mrs. S. Lawrence—902 Meridian
Mrs. E. L. Brown—522 E. Kingston
Mrs. F. Garner—909 Joe Wheeler's Ave.
Mrs. S. G. Wilson—802 S. 7th

MACOMB

HOTELS
Townsend—534 Summit St.
TOURIST HOMES
D. Mason—218 Denwidde St.

MERIDIAN

HOTELS
Beales—2411 Fifth St.
TOURIST HOMES
C. W. Williams—1208-31st St.
Mrs. H. Waters—1201 26th Ave.
Mrs. M. Simmons—5th St. betw. 16 & 17 A.
Charley Leigh—5th St. & 16th Ave.

MOUND BAYOU

TOURIST HOMES
Mrs. Sallie Price
Smith's
Mrs. Charlotte Strong
GARAGES
Liddle's

NEW ALBANY

HOTELS
Foot's—Railroad Ave.
TOURIST HOMES
S. Drewery—Church St.
Patt Knox—Cleveland St.
C. Morganfield—Cleveland St.

YAZOO CITY

HOTELS
Caldwell—Water & Broadway Sts.
TOURIST HOMES
Mrs. A. J. Walker—321 S. Monroe
Mrs. C. A. Wright—234 S. Yazoo

MISSOURI

CAPE GIRADEAU

TOURIST HOMES
G. Williams—408 S. Frederick St.
W .Martin—38 N. Hanover St.
J. Randol—422 North St.

CARTHAGE

TOURIST HOMES
Mrs. M. Webb—S. Fulton St.

COLUMBIA

HOTELS
Austin House—108 E. Walnut St.
TOURIST HOMES
Mrs. W. Harvey—417 N. 3rd St.

CHARLESTON

TAVERNS
Creole Cafe—311 Elm St.

EXCELSIOR SPRINGS

HOTELS
The Albany—408 South St.
Moore's—302 Maine St.

HANNIBAL

TOURIST HOMES
Mrs. E. Julius—1218 Gerard St.

JEFFERSON CITY

HOTELS
Lincoln—600 Lafayette St.
Booker T.
TOURIST HOMES
Miss C. Woodridge—418 Adams St.
R. Graves—314 E. Dunklin St.
RESTAURANTS
University—Lafayette & Dunklin Sts.
De Luxe—601 Lafayette St.
Blue Tiger—Chestnut & E Atchenson St.
College—905 E. Atchenson St.
BARBER SHOP
University—Lafayette & Dunklin St.
Tayes—Elm & Lafayette Sts.
BEAUTY PARLORS
Poro—818 Lafayette St.
SERVICE STATION
C. Little—Chestnut & Dunklin
TAVERNS
Tops—626 Lafayette St.
NIGHT CLUBS
Subway—600 Lafayette St.
Lone Star—930 E. Miller St.
TAXICABS
Veteran—515 Lafayette St.
TAILOR
Rightway—903 E. Atchenson St.

JOPLIN

HOTELS
Williams—308 Penna. St.
J. Lindsay—1702 Penna. St.
Mrs. F. Echols—901 Missouri Ave.
TOURIST HOMES
Mrs. Lindsay—1702 Penn. St.

KANSAS CITY

HOTELS
Booker T. Hotel—1823 Vine St.
Cadillac Hotel—1429 Forest
921 Hotel   921 East 17th Street
Watson—1211 S. Highland St.
Street's—1510 E. 18th St.
Lincoln Hotel—13th & Woodland Sts.
TOURIST HOMES
Mrs. Vallie Lamb—1914 E. 24th St.
Thomas Wilson—2600 Euclid Ave.
RESTAURANTS
Lill's Buffet—2458 Charlotte Ave.
Top Hat—1008 Garfield
Nashe's—1200 E. 18th St.
Oven—17th & Vine St.
Elnora's Cafe—1518 E. 18th St.
Dorothy's—2614 Prospect St.
Tasty Sandwich—1323½ E. 18th St.
Square Deal—1312 E. 15th St.
Porter's—1813 Vine
New Hollywood—907 E. 18th St.
TAVERNS
Vine St.—1519 E. 12th St.
NIGHT CLUBS
Chez Paree—1822 Vine St.
Scott's—2432 Vine St.
BEAUTY PARLORS
Hazel Graham—1836 Vine St.
Arlene—2409 Vine St.
Euthola—1602 E. 19th St.
Alexander—2429 Vine St.
Modern—1811½ Vine St.
LIQUOR STORES
Cardinal—1515 E. 18th St.
Monarch—2300 Prospect Ave.
Dundee—1701 Troost
Virginia—1601 Virginia
Chester's—18th & Charlotte St.
Golden Crown—2218 Vine
Ace—2404 Vine
Donnell—18th & Troost Sts.
SERVICE STATIONS
Stone's—2001 E. 31st St.
Mobile Station—1502 E. 19th St.
GARAGES
19th St.—1510 E. 19th St.
DRUG STORES
Community—2432 Vine St.
TAILORS
Spotless—2303 Prospect Ave.
COUNTRY CLUBS
Hillcrest—H'way 132 - 12 miles West of
  Kansas City

Penrod—H'way 40—13 milee W. of
Kansas City

LEBANON
TOURIST HOMES
Mrs. J.' Osborne—Rt. 5
Mrs. Ann Wilson—Rt. 3
Mrs. Eliza Turner—Rt. 3

MOBERLY
TOURIST HOMES
Mrs. F. Davis—212 N. Ault St.
Ralph Bass—517 Winchester St.
W. Johnson—N. 5th St. 400 blk.

POPLAR BLUFF
TOURIST HOMES
Mrs. W. Brooks—1800 N. Alice St.

SEDALIA
TOURIST HOMES
Mrs. T. L. Moore—505 W. Cooper
Mrs. C. Walker—217 E. Morgan
W. Williams—317 E. Johnson

SPRINGFIELD
TOURIST HOMES
U. G. Hardrick—238 Dollison Ave.

ST. JOSEPH
TOURIST HOMES
Mrs. T. J. Coleman—1713 Angelique St.

ST. LOUIS
HOTELS
Midtown—2935 Lawton Boulevard
Booker Washington—Jefferson at Pine
Poro—Pendleton & St. Ferdinand
West End—3900 W. Beele St.
Grand Central—Jefferson & Pine
Calumet—611 N. Jefferson Ave.
Corona—2840 Olive St.
Harlem—3438 Franklin
Antler—3502 Franklin Ave.

RESTAURANTS
Bob's—2816 Easton Avenue
Oak Leaf—4269 W. Easton Ave.
Society—900 N. Taylor Ave.-8
DeLuxe—10 N. Jefferson Ave.
Seashore—2829 Easton Ave.
Northside—2422 N. Pendleton Ave.
Lindsey's—3805 Page Blvd.
Snack Shop—1105 N. Taylor
Highway—1239 N. 20th St.
Wike's—1804 N. Taylor Ave.

BEAUTY PARLORS
Allen's—2343 Market St.
Shaw's—4356 Easton-13
Juvill—4141 Easton-13
Rosa's—1222 Armstrong
Artistic—1014 N. Whittier
Young's—2005 Pine St.
Artistic—909 N. Taylor-8

Azalie's—4621 Easton Ave.-13
Amanda's—1021 N. Cardinal Ave.-6
Ollie's—3803 Page Blvd.
Boulevard—1023 N. Grand Ave.-6
Parkway—4284 W. St. & Ferdinand-13
Argus—1008 N. Sarah St.
Hall's—3038 Franklin Ave.
Beauty Nook—3303 Lucas Ave.
Montgomery—3406 Franklin Ave.
Lottie's—3026 Lawton
Harris—919 Ohio Avenue
McCain—4702 A Newberry Terrace
Superior—219 A N. Jefferson
De Luxe—3604 Finnery Ave.
Clay's—613 N. 18th St.
2 Sisters—4126 Kennerly Ave.
Marcella—2306 Cole St.
Estrella's—4629 W. Aldine Ave.
Tillie's—2600 Cole St.

BARBER SHOPS
Bullock's—3320 Franklin Ave.

TAVERNS
Silver Slipper—2817 Easton Ave.
Glass Bar—2933 Lawton St.
Rio—18 South Jefferson
Carioca—1112 N. Sarah St.
Zanzibar—215 Cardinal-3
20th Century—718 N. Vanderventer-8
West End—939 N. Vanderventer Ave.
Hawaiian—3839 Finney Ave.
Play House—4071 Page Blvd.
Casablanca—4111 Finney Ave.
Manhattan—1115 N. Sarah
Zanzibar—215 N. Cardinal

NIGHT CLUBS
Paradise—930 N. Sarah St.
Riviera—4460 Delmar Blvd.
Sunset—6th & Peggot St.
West End—911 N. Vanderventer
Key—211 N. Cardinal Ave.-3
El Grotto—6412 Cottage Grove Ave.

SERVICE STATIONS
Midville—1913 Pendleton Ave.
Mac's—4102 Delmar
Anderson's—930 N. Compton
Merritt's—1701 Bond

GARAGES
Davis—3811 Finney Ave.
Fred Cooper's—Pine at Ewing Ave.

TAILORS
Jackson's—4501 W. Easton Ave.

LIQUOR STORES
Siegel's—1300 Franklin Ave.
K & F—3901 Olive St.
Harlem—4161 Easton Ave.
West End—937 N. Vanderventer Ave.

TAXICABS
Blue Jay—2811 Easton Ave.
DeLuxe—16 N. Jefferson Ave.

DRUG STORES
Taylor-Page—1301 N. Taylor
Douglas—3339 Laclede
Williams—2801 Cole St.
Harper's—3145 Franklin
Kinlock—Hugh St. & Carson Road
Ream's—1112 N. Sarah St.

EAST ST. LOUIS

HOTELS
Thigpin—1425 E. Broadway .

RESTAURANTS
Uutra-Modern—114 S. 15th St.
J. F. Sugg's—4305 Trendley Ave.
Del-Rio—1504 Broadway
Whiteway—4246 Market Ave.
Magnet—306 Broadway

BEAUTY PARLORS
Whitehead—8 N. 17th St.

SERVICE STATIONS
King's—1741 Bond Ave.

TAVERNS
Thigpin—1425 E. Broadway
South End—1527 Russell Ave.
Victory Club—4833 Tudor Ave.
Jolly Corner—1433 E. Broadway

TAILORS
Attucks—2217 Missouri Ave.

DRUG STORES
South End—1652 Central Ave.

MONTANA

HELENA

TOURIST HOMES
Mrs. M. Stitt—204 S. Park

NEBRASKA

FREMONT

C. M. Brannon—1550 N. C St.
Gus Henderson—1725 N. Irving St.

GRAND ISLAND

TOURIST HOMES
Mrs. M. Hunter—217 E. 5th St.

OMAHA

HOTELS
Broadview—2060 N. 19th St.
Patton—1014-18 S. 11th St.
Walker—2504 Charles St.
Willis—22nd & Willis

TOURIST HOMES
L. Strawther—2220 Willis Ave.
Mrs. M. Smith—2211 Ohio St.
Miss W. M. Anderson—2207 N. 25th St.
G. H. Ashby—2228 Willis Ave.
Dave Brown—2619 Caldwell St.

RESTAURANTS
Sharp Inn—2318 N. 24th St.
Neal's—N. 24th & Lake
Cozy—2615 No 24th St.

TAVERNS
Red Brick—2723 'Q' St.
Myrtis—2229 Lake St.
Len's—25th & Q St.
Apex—1818 N. 24th St.

NIGHT CLUBS
Railroad Men's—2701 N. 24th St.

LIQUOR STORES
Thrifty—24th & Lake St.
Crown—1512 N. 24th St.
Liquor—24th & Cumming

SERVICE STATIONS
Villone's—24th & Ohio
Gabby's—24th & Ohio
Kaplan—24th & Grant
Deep Rock—24th & Charles

DRUG STORES
Hermansky's—2725 Q St.
Duffy—24th & Lake St.
Johnson—2306 N. 24th St.
Reid's—24th & Seward Sts.

TAILORS
Tip Top—1804 N. 24th St.

LINCOLN

TOURIST HOMES
Mrs. E. Edwards—2420 'P' St.

RESTAURANTS
Roosevelt—610 N. 20th St.

BARBER SHOP
Service—237 N. 13th St.

DRUG STORE
Smith's—2146 Vine St.

TAILORS
Zimmerman—2355 O St.

NEW JERSEY

ASBURY PARK

TOURIST HOMES
Mrs. A. Arch—23 Atkins Ave.
Mrs. E. C. Burgess—1200 Springwood
Mrs. W. Greenlow—1317 Summerfield Ave.
Mrs. Brown—135 Ridge Ave.
Mrs. C. Jones—141 Sylvan Ave.
Mrs. V. Maupin—25 Atkins Ave.
E. C. Yeager—1406 Mattison Ave.
Anna Eaton—23 Atkins Ave.

HOTELS
Metropolitan—1200 Springwood
Reevy's—135 DeWitt Ave.
Whitehead—25 Atkins Ave.

RESTAURANTS
West Side—1136 Springwood Ave.
Nellie Fritts—Springwood Ave.
Tip Top Lunch—1143 Springwood Ave.
Nellie Tutt's—1207 Springwood Ave.

BEAUTY PARLORS
Imperial—1107 Springwood Ave.
Opal—1146 Springwood Ave.
Marions—1119 Springwood Ave.

BARBER SHOPS
Consolidated—1216 Springwood
John Milby—1216 Springwood Ave.

TAVERNS
Aztec Room—1147 Springwood Ave.
Capitol—1212 Springwood Ave.
Hollywood—1318 Springwood Ave.
2-Door—1512 Springwood Ave.

NIGHT CLUBS
Cuba's—Springwood Ave.

SERVICE STATIONS
Johnson—Springwood & DeWitt Place

GARAGES
Arrington—153 Ridge Ave.
West Side—1206 Springwood Ave.

ATLANTIC CITY

HOTELS
Liberty—1519 Baltic Avenue
Bay State—N. Tenn. Ave.
Randell—1601 Arctic Ave.
Ridley—1806 Arctic Ave.
Swan—136 N. Virginia Ave.
Wright—1702 Arctic Ave.
Capitol—37 N. Ky. Ave.
Lincoln—911 N. Indiana Ave.
Luzon—601 N. Ohio Ave.
Attucks—1120 Drexel Ave.
Apex Rest—Indiana & Ontario

TOURIST HOMES
A. R. S. Goss—324 N. Indiana Ave.
Mrs. V. Jones—1720 Arctic Ave.
M. Conte—111 N. Indiana Ave.
E. Satchell—27 N. Michigan Ave.
Bailey's Cottage—1812 Arctic Ave.
D. Austin—813 Baltic Ave.
R. Brown—113 N. Penn. Ave.

RESTAURANTS
Golden's—41 N. Kentucky Ave.
Little Diner—104 N. Kentucky Ave.
Smack Shack—40 N. Kentucky Ave.
Eddie's—1702 Arctic Ave.
Perry's—Kentucky Ave.
Young's—18 N. Ohio Ave.
Anderson's—1702 Arctic Ave.
Bedford's—Artic & S. Carolina Ave.
Kelly's—1311 Arctic Ave.

BARBER SHOPS
42 N. Illinois Ave.
Hollywood—811 Arctic Ave.
Hunter's—1814 Arctic Ave.

BEAUTY PARLORS
Mme. Newson's—225 N. Indiana Ave.
Grace's—43 Kentucky Ave.

TAVERNS
Wonder Bar—1601 Arctic Ave.
Little Belmont—37 N. Kentucky Ave.
Hattie's—1913 Arctic Ave.
Daddy Low's—Bay & Baltic Ave.
Mack's—1590 Baltic Ave.
Popular—1923 Artic Ave.
Elite—Baltic & Chalfonte Ave.
Herman's—Maryland & Artic
Prince's—37 N. Michigan Ave.
Austins—Maryland & Baltic
Golden's—41 N. Ky. Ave.
Elks Bar &Grill—1613 Artic
Lighthouse—1613 Baltic Ave.

New Jersey—N. J. & Mediterranean
Circus—37 N. Michigan Ave.
My Own—701 Baltic Ave.
Tim Buck Two—1600 Artic Ave.

NIGHT CLUBS
Harlem—32 N. Kentucky Ave.
Paradise—N. Illinois Ave.

LIQUOR STORES
Mark's—1923 Arctic Ave.
Timbucktu—1608 Arctic Ave.
Tumble Inn—Delaware & Baltic
Goodman's—1317 Arctic Ave.

SERVICE STATIONS
Mundy's—1814 Arctic Ave.

GARAGES
Johnson's—11-15 Ohio Ave.

DRUG STORES
London's—Cor. Ky. & Arctic Ave.

ATLANTIC HIGHLANDS

RESTAURANTS
Tennis Club Tea Room—Prospect Ave.

TAVERNS
New Way Inn—71 Ave. 'A'

BAYONNE

TAVERNS
Doc's—67 W. 23rd St.
John's—463 Ave 'C'
Golden Arrow—545 Hudson Blvd.

BELL MEADE

HOTELS
Bell Meade—Rt. 31

BRIDGESTON

TAVERNS
The Ram's Inn—Bridgeston & Millville Pike

CAMDEN

RESTAURANTS
Bar-B-Q—818 S. 9th St.

CHINESE RESTAURANTS
Lon's—806 Kaign Ave.

TAVERNS
Nick's—7th & Central Ave.

TAILORS
Merchant—741 Kaign Ave.

CAPE MAY

HOTELS
Richardson—Broad & Jackson Sts.
De Griff—833 Corgie St.

TOURIST HOMES
Mrs. M. Green—728 Lafayette St.

CEDAR KNOLL

COUNTRY CLUBS
The Shady Oak Lodge

EAST ORANGE
BEAUTY PARLORS
 The Ritz—214 Main St.
 Milan's—232 Halstead St.
TAILORS
 Vernon's—182 Amherst St.
 Charles—63 N Park St.

EATONTOWN
NIGHT CLUBS
 The Greenbriar—Pine Bush

EGG HARBOR
HOTELS
 Allen House—625 Cincinnati Ave.
TAVERNS
 Red, White & Blue Inn—701 Phila. Ave.

ELIZABETH
TOURIST HOMES
 Mrs. L. G. Brown—178 Madison St.
 Mrs. T. T. Davis—27 Dayton St.
TAVERNS
 Hunter's—1155 Dickerson St.
 One & Only—1112 Dickerson St.

ENGLEWOOD
TAVERNS
 The Lincoln—1-3 Englewood Ave.
LIQUOR STORES
 W. E. Beverage Co. 107 William St.
 Giles—107 Williams St.

HACKENSACK
BEAUTY PARLORS
 Mary—206 Central Ave.

HACK. 2-9733
5 POINT SERVICE STATION
SERVICE SUPREME
ESSO
Walter Levin, Prop.
First and Hackensack
Susquehanna St. N. J.

BARBER SHOPS
 Tip Top—174 Central Ave.
 Crosson—Railroad Place
TAVERNS
 Rideout's—204 Central Ave.

NIGHT CLUB
 Majestic Lodge—351 - 1st St.

HASKELL
RECREATION PARKS
 Thomas Lake

HIGHTSTOWN
TAVERNS
 Paul's Inn—Rt. 33 East Windsor TWP
 Old Barn—104 Daws St.

JERSEY CITY
BEAUTY PARLORS
 Beauty—74A Atlantic Ave.
TAILORS
 Bell's—630 Cummunipaw Ave.
 E. & E.—11A Oak St.

KINGSTON
ROAD HOUSES
 Merrill's

KEYPORT
TAVERNS
 Green Grove Inn—Atlantic & Halsey Street
 Major's—215 Atlantic Ave.

KENNELWORTH
TAVERNS
 Driver's—17th & Monroe Ave.

LAWNSIDE
TOURIST HOMES
 Hi-Hat—White Horse Pike
TAVERNS
 Acorn Inn—Whitehorse Pike
 Dreamland
 La Belle Inn—Gloucester Ave.
BEAUTY PARLORS
 Thelma Thomas—Warwick Blvd.
BARBER SHOPS
 Henry Smith—Mouldy Road
RECREATION PARKS
 Lawnside Park

LINDEN
NIGHT CLUBS
 4th Ward Club—1035 Baltimore
TAVERNS
 Victory—1307 Baltimore Avenue
TAILORS
 Quality—1140 E. St. George Ave.

LONG BRANCH
TAVERNS
 Club '45'—Liberty St.
 Sam Hall—18 Academy St.
 Tally Ho—185 Belmont Ave.

51

LAKEWOOD

BEAUTY SALON
Hollywood—17-4th St.

MADISON

TAXICABS
Madison—18 Lincoln Place
Yellow—14 Lincoln Place

MAHWAH

TAVERNS
Paul's Lunch—Brook St.

MOMOUTH JUNCTION

TOURIST HOMES
Macon's Inn—H'way Rt. No. 1-26

MONTCLAIR

SCHOOL OF BEAUTY CULTURE
Hair Dressing—207 Bloomfield Ave.
Scientfiic—146 Bloomfield Ave.
BARBER SHOPS
Paramount—211 Bloomfield Ave.
NIGHT CLUBS
Recreation—Glenridge Cor. Bay
GARAGES
Maple Ave.—80 Maple Ave.

MORRISTOWN

NIGHT CLUBS
Eureka—118 Spring St.

NEPTUNE

RESTAURANTS
Hampton Inn—1718 Sringwood Ave.
BEAUTY PARLORS
Priscilla's—261 Myrtle Ave.

NEWARK

HOTELS
Grand—78 W. Market St.
Y. M. C. A.—153 Court St.
Y. W. C. A.—20 Jones St.
Harwin Terrace—27 Sterling St.
TOURIST HOMES
Mrs. E. Morris—39 Chester Ave.
Mrs. Spence—506 Washington Ave.
RESTAURANTS
Cabin Grill—54 Waverly Ave.
Royal Palm—123 Waverly Ave.
Alpine—197 W. Kinney St.
Bar-B-Q—9 Monmouth St.
Easter—154 Prince St.
BEAUTY PARLORS
La Vogue—227 W. Kinney St.
Irene's 125 Somerset St.
Farrar—35 Prince St.
Billy's—206 Belmont Ave.
Chapman's—96 Belmont Ave.

BEAUTY PARLORS
Virginia Salon—132 West St.
Paris Salon—368 Washington St.
Dutcher's—156 Spruce St.
Mae's—271 Sringfield Ave.
Algene's—120 Spruce St.
Rene's—97 West St.
Queen—155 Barclay St.
BARBER SHOPS
Cochran's—323 Mulberry St.
El Idellio—30 Wright St.
TAVERNS
Bert's—211 Renner Ave.
Dodger's—8 Bedford Street
Dan's—245 Academy St.
Little Johnny's—47 Montgomery
Lestbaders—175 Spruce St.
Kesselman's—13th & Rutgers St.
Alcazar—72 Waverly Place
Rosen's—164 Spruce St.
Dave's—202 Court St.
Wtrren & Norfolk—256 Warren Stt.
Woods—258 Prince St.
Kleinbergs—88 Waverly St.
Afro—19 Quitman St.
Welcome Inn—87 West St.
Del Mar—133 Howard St.
'570'—570 Market St.
Boyd's—70 Boyd St.
Corprew's—297 Sprinfield Ave.
Dug-Out—188 Belmont Ave.
Harry's—60 Waverly Ave.
Ernie's—104 Wallace St.
Trippe's—121 Halstead St.
Mulberry—302 Mulberry St.
Frederick—2 Boston St.
NIGHT CLUBS
New Kinney Club—36 Arlington St.
Boston Plaza—4 Boston St.
Golden Inn—150 Charleston St.
Nest Club—Warren & Norfolk St.
Villa Maurice—375 Washington St.
Alcazar—72 Waverly Ave.
Picadilly—1 Peshine Tve.
Dodgers—8 Bedford St.
CHINESE RESTAURANTS
Chinese-American—603 W. Market
SERVICE STATIONS
Estes—39 Belmont Ave.
Livingston—300 W. Kinney St.
GARAGES
Branch—45 Rankin St.
TAILORS
I. Jordan—178 W. Kinney St.

OCEAN CITY

HOTELS
Washington—6th & Sampson Ave.

ORANGE

HOTELS
Y. M. C. A.—84 Oakwood Ave.
Y. W. C. A.—66 Oakwood Ave.
Oakwood Dep't—84 Oakland Ave.

RESTAURANTS
Triangle—152 Barrow St.
Jeter's—77 Barrow St.
Joe's—120 Barrow St.
Bar-B-Q—153 South St.
CHINESE RESTAURANTS
Orange Garden—157 Barrow St.
BEAUTY PARLORS
Park View—473 Central Ave.
Clarise—81 South St.
Elizabeth—159 South St.
Baugh—76 S. Center St.
Frank's—120 Hickory St.
NIGHT CLUBS
Paradise—Barrow & Chestnut St.
DRUG STORES
Bynum & Catlette—Barrow & Hickory St.
TAILORS
Fitchitt—99 Oakwood Ave.
Triangle—101 Hickory St.

PAULSBORO
RESTAURANTS
Elsie's—246 W. Adams St.

PATERSON
HOTELS
Joymakers—38 Bridge St.
TAVERNS
Idle Hour Bar—53 Bridge St.
Joymakers—38 Bridge St.
GARAGES
Brown's—57 Godwin St.

PERTH AMBOY
HOTELS
Lenora—550 Hartford St.
BARBER SHOPS
Kelly's—128 Fayette St.

POINT PLEASANT
TAVERNS
Joe's—337 Railroad Ave.

PINE BROOK
TOURIST HOMES
Wilson's
RESTAURANTS
Grigg's—58-60 Witherspoon St.
BEAUTY PARLORS
Vanity Box—188 John St.

PLAINFIELD
TAVERNS
Liberty—4th St.

PLEASANTVILLE
TAVERNS
Harlem Inn—1117 Washington Ave.
ROAD HOUSES
Martin's—304 W. Wright St.

RAHWAY
ROAD HOUSE
O. Paterson—Edwards Ave. & Potters Crossing

RED BANK
HOTELS
Robins Rest—615 River Road
RESTAURANTS
Vincents—263 Shrewsbury Ave.
Dan Logan's—W. Bergen Place
TAVERNS
West Bergen—103 W. Bergen Place
Charlie's—W. Bergen Place
BARBER SHOPS
A. Dillard—250 Shrewsbury Ave.
BEAUTY PARLORS
R. Alleyne—124 W. Bergen Place
Suries—214 Shrewsbury Ave.
SERVICE STATIONS
Galatres—Shrewsbury & Catherine
TAILORS
Dudley's—79 Sunset Ave.

ROSELLE
TAVERNS
Omega—302 E. 9th St.
St. George—1139 St. George Ave.

SCOTCH PLAINS
RESTAURANTS
Hill Top—60 Jerusalem Road
ROAD HOUSES
Villa Casanova—Jerusalem Road
COUNTRY CLUBS
Shady Rest—Jerusalem Road

SALEM
TAVERNS
Stith's—111 Market St.

SEA BRIGHT
RESTAURANTS
Castle Inn—11 New Street

SHREWSBURY
SERVICE STATIONS
Rodney's—Shrewsbury Ave.

SUMMIT
HOTELS
Y. M. C. A.—393 Broad St.

TOMS RIVER
TAVERNS
Casaloma—Manitan Park

TRENTON
HOTELS
Y. M. C. A.—105 Spring St.

TOURIST HOMES
Mrs. C. Taylor—92 Spring St.
Mrs. M. Morris—116 Spring St.
Mrs. Pleash—88 Spring St.
Mrs. Garland—62 Spring St.

RESTAURANTS
Spot Sandwich—121 Spring St.

BEAUTY PARLORS
Bea's—83 Spring St.
Geraldine's—17 Trent St.

BARBER SHOPS
Sanitary—199 N. Willow St.
Bill's—81 Spring St.

NIGHT CLUBS
Famous—228 N. Willow Street

ROAD HOUSE
Crossing Inn—Eggertt's Crossing

POOL PARLOR
Reid's—219 Fall St.

VAUX HALL

BEAUTY PARLORS
Celeste—211 Springwood Ave.

TAVERNS
Carnegie—380 Carnegie Place

ROAD HOUSES
Lloyd Chicken Farm—26 Valley

WILDWOOD

HOTELS
Glen Oak—100 E. Lincoln St.
The Marion—Artic & Spicer Ave.
Artic Ave.—3600 Artic Ave.

TOURIST HOMES
The Denmond—129 W. Spicer Ave.
Mrs. A. H. Brown—3811 Artic
Mrs. E. Crawley—3816 Artic

RESTAURANTS
Palm Leaf—3812 Artic Ave.

BEAUTY PARLORS
B. Johnson's—407 Garfield Ave.

BARBER SHOPS
R. Morton—4010 New Jersey Ave.

NIGHT CLUBS
High Steppers—437 Lincoln Ave.

WOODSBURY

RESTAURANTS
Robinson's—225 Park Ave.

WEST PLEASANTVILLE

COUNTRY CLUB
Pine Acres Country Club—Atlantic City

NEW YORK STATE

ALBANY

HOTELS
Broadway—603 Broadway

TOURIST HOMES
Mrs. Aaron J. Oliver—42 Spring St.

RESTAURANTS
Broadway—603 Broadway

BEAUTY PARLORS
Buelah Fords—96 2nd St.

BARBER SHOPS
Martin's—4 Vantromp St.

SERVICE STATIONS
Ten Eyck—137 Lark St.

NIGHT CLUBS
Harlem Grill—Hamilton St.
Rythm Club—Madison Ave.

BUFFALO

HOTELS
Little Harlem—494 Michigan Ave.
Y. M. C. A.—585 Michigan Ave.
Montgomery—486 Michigan Ave.
Vendome—177 Clinton St.
Claridge—38 Broadway

TOURIST HOMES
Miss R. Scott—244 N. Division St.
Mrs. F. Washington—172 Clinton St.
Mrs. G. Chase—192 Clinton St.
William Campbell—22 Milnor

RESTAURANTS
Horseshoe—198 Pine St.
Lou's—154 Williams St.
Rozer's—Williams & Bennett
Crystal—534 Broadway
Bar-B-Q—413 Michigan Ave.
Empire—454 Michigan Ave.
Silver Star—175 Williams
Elite—168 Clinton
Alma's—314 Williams
Chet & Als—486 William St.
Standard—66 Ridge St.
Pepper Pot—377 Jefferson St.
Apex—311 William St.
Arnold's—348 William St.

CHINESE RESTAURANTS
Kam Wing Loo—433 Michigan Ave.

BEAUTY PARLORS
Orchid—419 Pratt St.
Melisey's—236 William St.
Artisian—271 Spring St.
La Ritz—348 Jefferson Ave.
Matchless—169 William St.
Edwards—530 William St.
Lady Esther 243 E. Ferry St.
Jean's—142 Adams St.
La Grace—620 Brodway
Laura's—643 Broadway
Rena's—494 Jefferson Ave.
Modern's—170 Clinton St.
La Mae—437 Jefferson Ave.
Jessie's—560 Spring St.

BARBER SHOPS
Elite—171 William St.
People's—433 Williams St.

TAVERNS
Pearls—474 Michigan Ave.
Clover Leaf—443 Michigan Ave.
Jefferson—381 Jefferson
Apex—311 Williams St.

TAVERNS
Hickory—Hickory & Williams
Horse Shoe—Williams & Pine
Little Harlem—496 Michigan
Toussaint—292 Williams St.
Joe's—416 William St.
Tuxedo—121 Williams St.
Glass Horseshoe—214 Williams St.
Jamboree—339 Williams St.
Mandy's—278 Williams St.
Polly's—483 Jefferson St.

NIGHT CLUBS
Moonglow—Michigan & Williams
Jamboree—339 Williams
Cotton Club—349 Broadway

LIQUOR STORES
Zarin—557 Clinton St.
Parkside—452 William St.
Swan—Swan & Hickory St.
Aqui-Line—141 Broadway
Ferry—192 E. Ferry St.
Totton's—344 Jefferson Ave.
Stenson's—133 William St.

SERVICE STATIONS
Fraas—Clinton & Jefferson
Burns—120 Willilams St.
Spring St.—240 Spring St.
Oab's—90 Williams St.
Al's—Clinton & Enslie Sts.
Klein's—Clinton & Emslie St.

TAILORS
Twi-Light—458 Williams St.
Eagle—414 Eagle St.
Reeve's—119 Clinton St.
Mickey's—541 Williams St.
Shirley's 533 Broadway
Tidwell—561 Eagle St.

TAXICAB
Veteran—63 William St.

ELMIRA

HOTELS
Wilson—307 E. Clinton St.
TOURIST HOMES
J. A. Wilson—307 E. Clinton St.

ITHACA

NIGHT CLUBS
Forest City Lodge—119 S. Tioga St.

GLEN FALLS

TOURIST HOMES
Mrs. M. Mayberry—16 Ferry St.

JAMESTOWN

TOURIST HOMES
Mrs. I. W. Herald—51 W. 10th St.
Mrs. J. M. Brown—108 W. 11th St.

LACKAWANNA

RESTAURANTS
Little Swan—25 Wasson Ave.
Standard—68 Ridge Road

Chicken Shack—23 Simon Ave.
Merriweathers—73 Ridge Rd.
TAVERNS
Little Harlem—26 Gates Ave.

NIAGARA FALLS

TOURIST HOMES
Mack-Hayes House—437 1st St.
Mrs. Alice Ford—413 Main St.
Fairview—413 Main St.
Mrs. Brown—1202 Haeberie Ave.
Parker House—627 Erie Avenue
A. E. Gabriel—635 Erie Ave.
C. A. Brown—3106 Highland Ave.

BARBER SHOPS
Garland—Erie Ave.

TAVERNS
Sunset Cafe—619 Erie Ave.
Chef. W. Martin—609 Erie Ave.
Cephas—621 Erie Ave.
Andrew's—135 Memorial Park

GARAGES
Smith & Bradberry—150 Memorial P'kway.

PORT JERVIS

TOURIST HOMES
R. Pendleton—26 Bruce St.

POUGHKEEPSIE

TOURIST HOMES
Mrs. S. Osterholt—16 Crannell St.
Mrs. S. Le Fever—217 Union St.
G. W. Hayes—93 N. Hamilton

ROCHESTER

HOTELS
Gibson—461 Clariss St.
Freeman House—112 Industrial St.
TOURIST HOMES
G. W. Burke—221 Columbia Ave.
Mrs. Latimer—179 Clarissa St.
NIGHT CLUBS
Cotton Club—222 Joseph Avenue

SCHENECTADY

HOTELS
Clefton—516 Broadway
TOURIST HOMES
R. Rhinehart—125 S. Church St.
S. Kearney—857 McDonald Ave.
G. D. Thomas—123 S. Church St.

SYRACUSE

HOTELS
The Savoy—518 E. Washington St.
Almond House—210 Almond St.
TOURIST HOMES
W. R. Farrish—809 E. Faytte. St.
RESTAURANTS
Little Harlem—449 E. Washington St.
Aunt Edith's—601½ Harrison St.
Field's—E. Adams & S. Townsend St.

TAVERNS
  Penquin—822 S. State St.
BARBER SHOPS
  Cameron—401 E. Washington St .
  Smith's—600½ E. Washington St.
NIGHT CLUBS
  Goldie's—423 Harrison St.
LIQUOR STORE
  Mulroy's—301 E. Genesse St.
GARAGES
  Ben's—829 S. Townsend St.
DRUG STORES
  Allen's—928 S. Townsend St.

UTICA
TOURIST HOMES
  Broad St. Inn—415 Broad St.
  Mrs. S. Burns—318 Broad St.
  Howard Home—413 Broad St.

WATERTOWN
TOURIST HOMES
  E. F. Thomas—123 Union St.
  V. H. Brown—502 Binase St.
  G. E. Deputy—711 Morrison St.

NEW YORK CITY
(HARLEM)

Cambridge—141 W. 10th St.
El-Melrab—21 W. 135th St.
Martha—6 W. 135th St.
Garrett House—314 W. 127th St.
Press—23 W. 135th St.
The Viola—227 W. 135th St.

HOTELS
CROSSTOWN HOTEL
515 WEST 145th STREET
The Tenrub—328 St. Nicholas
Elks—608 St. Nicholas
Beakford—300 W. 116th St.
Braddock—126th & 8th Ave.
Theresa—125th St. & 7th Ave.
Grampion—182 St. Nicholas
Olgo—695 Lenox Ave.
Woodside—2424 7th Ave.

Y. M. C. A.—180 W. 135th St.
Y. W. C. A.—175 W. 137th St.
Currie—101 W. 145th St.
Mariette—170 W. 121st St.
Cecil—208 W. 118th St.
Revella—307 W. 116th St.

HOTELS
Barbera—501 West 142 St.

Brown's—210 W. 135th St.
E & M—2016 7th Ave.
Em & Bee—458 Lenox Ave.
Davis'—2066 7th Ave.

Harris' Corner—132nd & 7th Ave.
Little Shack—2267 7th Ave.
Elsie's—975 St. Nicholas Ave.
Doris'—2066 7th Ave.

RESTAURANTS
Otis Coles—108 West 145th St.
Jimmie's Chicken Shack—763 St. Nicholas A.
Pete's—2534 8th Ave.
Virginia—271 W. 119th St.
Clarkson Bros.—2499 - 7th Ave.
Lulu Belle—229 W. 125th St.
Pete's Creole Restaurant—2230 7th Ave.
Bob's Lounge—2165 8th Ave.
Lulu Belle's—317 W. 126th St.
Four Star—2433 7th Ave.
Jim's Cuban Lunchionette—2346 8th Ave.
RITZ TEAROOM
2310—7th AVENUE
"The Squeeze Inn"—2125-7th Ave.
Helen's Haven—2930 8th Ave.
Pauline's—1627 Amsterdam Ave.
Tabb's—2354 7th Ave.
Watson's—127 Lenox Ave.
El Mundial—2201 7th Ave.
James Bar-B-Q—1815 Amsterdam Ave.
Esquire Lunchonette—2201 7th Ave.
Bee Bee's Blueplate—2373-7th Ave.
Al's—57 Lenox Ave.
Sherman's Bar-B-Q—1835 Amsterdam Ave.

Empire—125th St. & Lenox Ave.
Jimmy's—763 St. Nicholas Ave.

RESTAURANTS
Gertrude's—267 West 141st St.
Four Star—2433 - 7th Ave.
George's—1921 Amsterdam Ave.
Jennie Lou's—2297 - 7th Ave.
Hamburg Paradise—377 West 125th St.
Bodden & Clark—2150 - 7th Ave.

CHINESE RESTAURANT
Mayling—1723 Amsterdam Ave.

BEAUTY PARLORS
Elite—2544-7th Ave.
Myers & Griffin—65 W. 134th St.
Your Pal—22 W. 133rd St.
National—301 W. 144th St.
Neuway—143 W. 116th St.
A. L. Smith—2411 7th Ave.
Oneda's—231 Edgecombe Ave.
Sibley's—301 W. 126th St.
Beard's—322 St. Nicholas Ave.
Bonnie's—165 W. 127th St.
Dorothy's—247 West 144th St.
Rose Meta's—148th St. & St. Nicholas Ave.
Lillette's—1308 Amsterdam Ave.

BARBER SHOPS
Sportsmen's Barber Shop—2224-7th Ave.
Davis—69 W. 138th St.

DE LUX
90 St. Nicholas Place
The Best On The Hill
James Monroe, Mgr.—Tel. AU 3-9186

Renaissance—2349 7th Ave.
DeLux—2799 8th Ave.
WORLD BARBER SHOP
2621 - 8th AVENUE
Bob Cary's—2521 8th Ave.
Spooner's—2435 8th Ave.
DUNBAR BARBER SHOP
2808—8th AVENUE
B. Garrett—2311 7th Ave.
Eldorado—203 W. 116th St.
Hi-Hat—2276 7th Ave.
Hoghie Rayford—2013 7th Ave.
IDEAL BARBER SHOP
716 ST. NICHOLAS AVENUE
Leon & Eddie's—353 W. 145th St.
Roxy—2322 7th Ave.
Modernistic—2132 7th Ave.
Service—7th Ave. & 135th St.

TAVERNS
Lenox Lounge—290 Lenox Ave.
El Favorito Bar—2055 Eighth Ave.
Old Time Tavern—2160 5th Ave.
International—2150 5th Ave.
GOLDEN BAR & GRILL
366 WEST 145th STREET
Arthur's—2481 8th Ave.

Red Tip—2470-7th Avenue
Bird Cage—2308 7th Ave.
John Allen's—207 W. 116th St.
Brittwood—594 Lenox Ave.
POP'S BAR & LOUNGE
1981 AMSTERDAM AVENUE
Big Apple—2300 7th Ave.
Frank Lezama—3578 Broadway
Frankie's Cafe—2328-7th Ave.
Bank's—2338 - 8th Ave.
Paradise—2033-8th Ave.
JENNINGS BAR & GRILL
Cor. Amsterdam Ave. & 162nd St.
Little Zhack—2267 - 7th Ave.
Ray's—165th St. & Broadway

HARRIS' CORNER
PHONES: AU3-8445—3-8155
132nd Street & 7th Avenue
Featuring—
Chicken In The Rough
SHRIMPS — SCALLOPS
Best of Wines and Liquors
PERCY R. HARRIS, PROP.

Shalimar—3638 Broadway
Palm—209 West 125th St.
Frank's—313 West 125th St.
Covan's—371 West 125th St.
Renny—2359 - 7th Ave.
Parkway—2063 - 8th Ave.
Dolen-Taylor—134 Hamilton Place
S. S. Francois—2104 - 7th Ave.
Chick's—2501 - 7th Ave.
C. L. D. - 1948 - 7th Ave.
Mac's—267 West 125th St.
William's—2011 - 7th Ave.

BROWNIE'S
2571—8th AVE. —— 2557—8th AVE.
Choice Wines, Liquors & Beer
AU 3-9761   Janice Brown, Prop.

Dawn—1931 Amsterdam Ave.
Pasadena—2350 - 8th Ave.
Barfield—2379 - 7th Ave.
Joe Louis—11 West 125th St.
Jack Carters—1890 - 7th Ave.
Poor John's—2268 - 8th Ave.

Baby Grand—319 West 125th St.

Al's—415 West 125th St.
Horseshoe—2474 - 7th Ave.
Lou's—1985 Amsterdam Ave.
Welcome Inn—2895 - 8th Ave.
Dick Wheaton's—7th Ave. & 137th St.

Blue Heaven—378 Lenox Ave.
Calvacade—2104 7th Ave.
Colonial—116 Bradhurst Ave.

TAVERNS
Eddie's—714 St. Nicholas Ave.
Elk Scene—469 Lenox Ave.

Hot-Cha—2280 7th Ave.
Jay's—400 W. 148th St.
La Mar Cheri—739 St. Nichollas Ave.
Logas—2496 7th Ave.
Monte Carlo—2247 7th Ave.
Murrain—635 Lenox Ave.
Orange Blossom—570 Lenox Ave.
Speedway—92 St. Nicholas Ave.
Victoria—2418 7th Ave.
721 St. Nicholas Ave. Grill
Fat Man—St. Nicholas Ave. & 155th St.
Mayfair—773 St. Nicholas Ave.
C. L. D. Grill—1958-7th Ave.
Jimmie Daniels—114 W. 116th St.
Chick's—2501 7th Ave.
Moon Glow—2461 7th Ave.
Palm Cafe—209 W. 125th St.

Palace Bar & Grill—247 Lenox
George Farrell's—2711 8th Ave.
Novelty Bar & Grill—1965 Amsterdam Ave.
Johnson's—614 Lenox Ave.
L-Bar—3601 Broadway
Chick's Bar & Grill—2501 7th Ave.
Well's Cocktail Bar—2249 7th Ave.
Sport's Inn—2308 8th Ave.
The Colonial—2321 8th Ave.
Clover Bar & Grill 1735 Amsterdam Ave.
Swanky Bar & Grill—1744 Amsterdam Ave.
Welcome Inn—2895 8th Ave.
Lou's—1985 Amsterdam Ave.
Daniel"s—2461 7th Ave.

THE TALK OF THE TOWN

Little Alpha Service

THE COMPLETE CLEANERS

200 WEST 136th STREET

(NEAR 7th AVENUE)

Phone: AU 3-0671

6 - 8 HOUR SERVICE

ONE OF NEW YORK'S PIONEER CLEANERS

R.E EUBANKS. MGR.

TAVERNS
Horseshoe—2474 7th Ave.
Mac's—267 W. 125th St.
Coran's—2359 7th Ave.

Tel: UN 4-8577

HARLEM

BAR and GRILL

Visit Our

Newly Decorated "U" Bar

Dine In The Avenue's Only
Fountain Cocktail Lounge

MODERATE PRICES———
———SATISFACTORY SERVICE

2140—7th Avenue   Cor. 127th St.

Parkway—2063 8th Ave.
Pelican—45 Lenox Ave.
Bar '61'—61 W. 125th St.
Jock's—2350 7th Ave.
Randolph's Shangri La—1978 Amsterdam Av.
Mandalay—2201 7th Ave.
Broadway Palace—147th & Broadway
Williams'—2011 7th Ave.
Bell's Bar—Broadway & 149th St.
Dawn Cafe—1931 Amsterdam Ave.
Old Pasadena—2350 8th Ave.
Chateau Lounge—379 W. 125th St.
Jerry's Bar—2091-8th Ave.
NIGHT CLUBS
Small's Paradise—2294 7th Avve.
Elk's Rendezvous—133rd & Lenox Ave.
Celebrity Club—35 E. 125th St.

NIGHT CLUBS
Murrain's—132nd & 7th Ave.
Caribbean Club—2387 7th Ave.
Hollywood Club—116th & Lenox Ave.
Lenox Rendezvous—75 Lenox Ave.
Club Sudan—640 Lenox Ave.
Hollywood—105 West 116th St., N. Y. C.
Club Baron—132nd St. & Lenox Ave.

LIQUOR STORES
Friedland's—605 Lenox Ave.
J & D—271 West 141st St.

Call AU 3-8340

Free Prompt Delivery

WE RECOMMEND

GOLDMAN'S

WINES AND Liquors

New York State Retail Wine
& Liquor Store License·L-761

483 W. 155th St. — New York

Corner Amsterdam Avenue

LIQUOR STORES
Square Wine & Liquor—209 W. 127th St.
Leslie T. Turner—26 Macombs Place
Margaret B. Gray—394 Manhattan Ave.
Dave's—472 Lenox Ave.

60

GARAGES
  Viaduct—101 Macombs Place
  Colonial Park—310 W. 144th St.
  Polo Grounds—155th St. & St. Nicholas Ave.
  McClary's—163 West 132nd St.
AUTOMOTIVE
  The New Deal—30 W. 140th St.
TAILORS

  Robert Lewis—1980-7th Ave.
  La Fontaine—470 Convent Ave.
  Broadway—92 St. Nicholas Ave.

DANCE HALLS
  Savoy—Lenox Ave. & 140th St.
  Golden Gate—Lenox Ave. & 142nd St.

BROOKLYN

HOTELS
  Y. M. C. A.—405 Carlton Ave.
  Norma—145 Gates Ave.
  T. C. U.—1124 Fulton St.

RESTAURANTS
  Dew Drop—363 Halsey St.
  El Rose—1093 Fulton St.
  Little Roxy—490A Summer Ave.
  Bernice's Cafeteria—105 Kingston Ave.
  Spick & Span—70 Kingston Ave.
BEAUTY PARLORS
  Bartley's—1125 Fulton St.
  Lamae—545 Classon Ave.
  Katerine's—345 Sumner Ave.
  Ideal—285-A Sumner Ave.
SCHOOLS OF BEAUTY CULTURE
  Theresa—301 Livonia Ave.

TAVERNS
  Palm Gardens—491 Summer Ave.
  Royal—1073 Fulton St.
  Goodwill—1942 Fulton St.
  Parkside—759 Gates Ave.
  Stuyvesant—Hancock & Lewis Ave.
  Capitol Bar—1550 Fulton St.
  Turner's—1698 Fulton St.
  Decatur Bar & Grill—301 Reid Ave.
  Kingston Tavern—1496 Fulton St.
  Arlington Inn—1253 Fulton St.
  McGorem's—1253 Bedford Ave.
  Gallagher's Bar—249 Reid Ave.
  Kingston Lounge—Kingston Cor. Bergen
  Rainbow Inn—1630 Fulton St.
  Durkin Tavern—1289 Fulton St.
  Disler's—759 Gates Ave.
  Elegant Bar & Grill—1420 Fulton St.
  Verona Leafe—1330 Fulton St.
  Frank's—Kingston & Atlantic Ave.
  K & C Tavern—588 Gates Ave.
  George's—328 Tompkins Ave.
  Smitty's—286 Patchen Ave.
  Casablanca—300 Reid Ave.
  Tropic Moon—1304 Fulton St.
  Buckham's—399 Nostrand Ave.
  Ten-Twelve—Sumner & Myrtle Aves.
  Bedford Rest—1253 Bedford Ave.
  Country Cottage—375 Franklin Ave.
  Bombay—377 Christopher St.
  Bedford Lounge—1194 Fulton St.
  Marion's—125 Marion St.
  Capitol—1550 Fulton St.
  Corba—1593 E. New York Ave.
NIGHT CLUBS
  Hanlew—334 Lewis St.
  Lion's—307 Ralph Ave.
WINE & LIQUOR STORES
  Yak—1361 Fulton St.
  Lincoln—401 Tompkins Ave.
  York—1361 Fulton St.
  Stuyvesant—1551 Fulton St.
  Gottlesman's—41 Albany St.
  Allen Rose—106 Kingston Ave.
  Turner's—249 Sumner St.
  Gottesman's—41 Albany Ave.
  Sexton's—616 Halsey St.
TAILORS
  G & O—84 Troy Ave.

For Comfort and Service

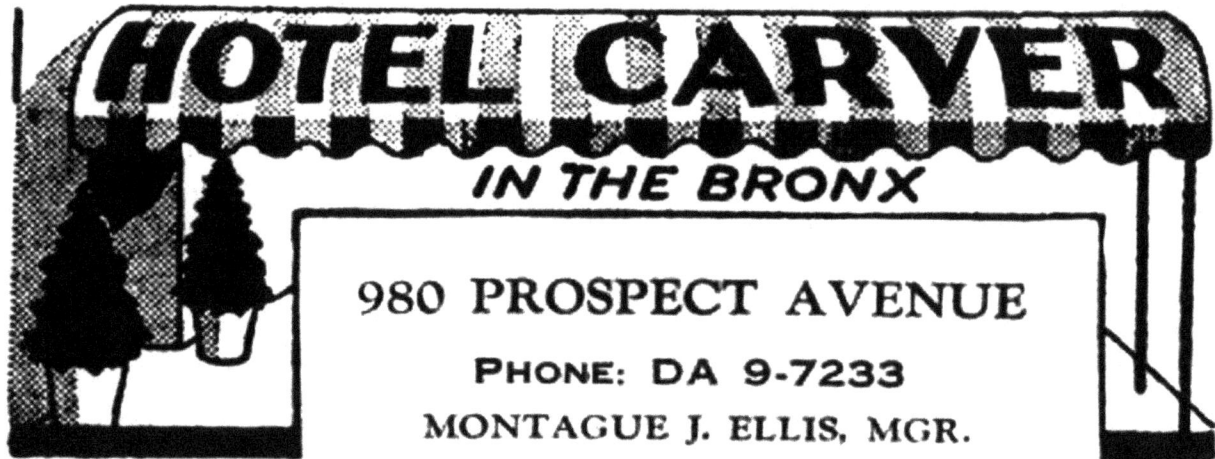

HOTEL CARVER
IN THE BRONX

980 PROSPECT AVENUE
PHONE: DA 9-7233
MONTAGUE J. ELLIS, MGR.

(BRONX)

HOTELS
Carver—980 Prospect Ave.

RESTAURANTS
Fischer's—1086 Boston Road
Betty's Blue Room—1363 Stebbins Ave.
The Blue Way—3269 3rd Ave.
Dick's—699 E. 163rd St.
Denton's—1300 Boston Road
Shrimp's—734 East 165th St.
Daniel's—1107 Prospect Ave.

BEAUTY PARLORS
Grayson—974 Prospect Ave.
Glennada—875 Longwood Ave.

TAVERNS
Freddie's Cafe—1204 Boston Road
Uncle Curley's—3589 Third Ave.
Prospect Cafe—845 Prospect Ave.
The Fair Play—1260 Boston Road
Boston Road Cafe—1078 Boston Road
Sun Brite 921 Prospect Ave.
Harty's Mid-Way—458 E. 165th St.
Louis' Ambosino—737 E. 165th St.
Neighborhood—3344 Third Ave.
Third Ave. Rendezvous—3377 Third Ave.
Prospect Bar & Grill 1431 Prospect Ave.
Louis' Tavern—3510 Third Ave.
Kennie's—853 Freeman St.
Lucille's—3800 Third Ave.
Jimmy's—267 E. 161st St.
Zombie Bar—1745 Boston Road
Rainbow Gardens—977 Prospect Ave.
The Forest Lounge—750 E. 165th St.
Boston Road Tavern—1429 Prospect Ave.
Johnny's—1048 Boston Road
B & P—823 E. 169th St.
Trinity—163rd & Trinity Ave.
Ralph Rida's—1155 Tinton Ave.
Triangle—849 E. 169th St.
Old Harlem Union Cafe—1087 Union Ave.
Rendez-Vous—907 Prospect Ave.

Bronxwood—3950 Bronxwood Ave.
Crystal Lounge—1035 Prospect Ave.
Happy Hour—1183 Boston Road
Four Aces—1306 Boston Road

TAVERNS
Central—271 East 161st Street
Kelly's—430 East 169th St.
Fair Play—1260 Boston Road
Kennie's—853 Freeman St.
Prospect—1431 Prospect Ave.
Step Inn—1308 Washington Ave.
Five Corners—169th St. & Boston Road
Third Ave.—3377 - 3rd Ave.
Freddie's—1204 Boston Road
Uncle Curley's—3589 3rd Ave.
Sporting Life—950 Prospect Ave.
Louis Ambrosino—737 East 165th St.
Central—267 East 161st St.
DeLuxe—270 East 161st St.
Johnny's—1056 Boston Road
Elk's—980 Prospect Ave.
Midway—458 East 165th St.
Forest Lounge—750 East 165th St.
Boston Road—1078 Boston Road
Rendezvous—907 Prospect Ave.
Hilltop—947 Forest Ave.
Trinity—163rd St. & Trinity Ave.
SunBrite—921 Prospect Ave.
Hi-Spot—3824 - 3rd Ave.

WINE & LIQUORS
Franklin Ave.—1214 Franklin Ave.
Prospect—889 Prospect Ave.
Jack's—1309 Prospect Ave.
West Farms—2026 Boston Road
O'Connell's—1311 Boston Road
Prospect—889 Prospect Ave.

NIGHT CLUBS
845—845 Prospect Ave.

BALLROOM
McKinley—1258 Boston Road

62

TAILORS
  Hendrix's—1202 Union Ave.
  DeLux—857 Freeman St.

LONG ISLAND

AMITYVILLE
RESTAURANTS
  Watervliet—158 Dixon Ave.
ROAD HOUSE
  Freddy's—Albany & Banbury Court
BARBER SHOP
  Jimmy's—Albany & Brewster
BEAUTY PARLORS
  Boyd's—21 Banbury Court

CORONA
TAVERNS
  Big George—106 Northern Blvd.
  Prosperity—32-19 103rd St.
NIGHT CLUBS
  New Cameo—108 Northern Blvd.

FLUSHING
ROAD HOUSE
  Club Forty—40 Lawrence St.

HEMPSTEAD
TAVERNS
  Eddie Bar & Grill—28 S. Franklin

JAMAICA
TAVERNS
  Tolliver's—112 New York Blvd.
  Hank's—108 New York Blvd.
BEAUTY PARLORS
  Roslyn—106 New York Blvd.
TAILORS
  Klugh's—109 Union Hall St.
  Merit—109 Merrick Blvd.

WESTCHESTER

ELMSFORD
TAVERNS
  Clarke—91 Saw Mill River Road

MT. VERNON
RESTAURANTS
  Hamburger Bar—15 W. 3rd St.
  Southern Tea Room—44 W. 3rd St.
  Friendship—50 W. 3rd St.
SCHOOL OF BEAUTY CULTURE
  Orchid—48 W. 3rd St.
TAVERNS
  Mohawk Inn—142 S. 7th Ave.
  Friendship Center—50 W. 3rd St.
  Golden Lion—50 S. 8th St.

NEW ROCHELLE
RESTAURANTS
  City Park—521 5th Ave.
  Harris—29 Morris St.
  Week's—68 Winyah Ave.

BEAUTY PARLORS
  A. Berry—50 DeWitts Place
  B. Miller—8 Brook Ave.
  Ocie—41 Rochelle Place
BARBER SHOPS
  The Royal Salon—4 Brook Ave.
  Field's—66 Winyah Ave.
  Bal-Mo-Ral—56 Brook St.
LIQUOR STORE
  A. Edwards—112 Union Ave.
DRUGGIST
  Daniels—57 Winyah Ave.

NORTH CASTLE
ROAD HOUSE
  Carolina Lodge

OSSINING
BEAUTY PARLOR
  Leona's—13 Hunter St.

NORTH TARRYTOWN
BARBER SHOPS
  Lemon's—Valley St.
  J. Brown—Valley St.
BEAUTY PARLOR
  J. Prioleau—88 Valley St.

TUCKAHOE
RESTAURANTS
  Major's—48 Washington St.
  Butterfly Inn—47 Washington St.
BEAUTY PARLORS
  Shanhana—144 Main St.
BARBER SHOPS
  Al's—144 Main St.

WHITE PLAINS
RESTAURANTS
  Carver Lunch—168 Whitfield St.

YONKERS
TAVERNS
  The Brown Derby—125 Nepperham Ave.

NEW MEXICO
ALBUQUERQUE
TOURIST HOMES
  Mrs. W. Bailey—1127 N. 2nd St.
RESTAURANTS
  Bon Ton—115 N. First St.

CARLSBAD
TOURIST HOMES
  Mrs. A. Sherrell—502 S. Haloquens
  L. M. Smith—514 South Canyon

DEMING
TOURIST HOMES
  M. Wilson—Iron & 2nd St.

LASCRICES

TOURIST HOMES
Mrs. R. B. McCoy—545 N. Church

ROSWELL

TOURIST HOMES
Mrs. Mary Collins—121 E. 10th St.
R. Brown—115 E. Walnut St.

RESTAURANTS
Sunset Cafe—115 E. Walnut St.

TUCMCARI

TOURIST HOMES
Rockett Inn—524 N. Campbell St.

NORTH CAROLINA

ASHEVILLE

HOTELS
Y. W. C. A.—360 College St.
Booker T. Washington—409 Southside Ave.
Savoy—Eagle & Market St.

RESTAURANTS
Palace Grille—19 Eagle St.

BEAUTY PARLORS
Butler's—Eagle & Market St.

BARBER SHOPS
Wilson's—13 Eagle St.

TAVERNS
Wilson's—Eagle & Market Sts.

GARAGES
Wilkin's—Eagle & Market Sts.

BLADENBORO

BEAUTY PARLORS
Lacy's Beauty Shop

CARTHAGE

HOTELS
Carthage Hotel

CHARLOTTE

SERVICE STATIONS
Bishop Dale—First & Brevard Sts.

DURHAM

HOTELS
Biltmore—E. Pettigrew St.
Jones—502 Ramsey St.

RESTAURANTS
Congo Grill—Pettigrew St.
Catlett's—1502 Pettigrew St.
Elivira's—801 Fayetteville St.

BEAUTY PARLORS
De Shazors—809 Fayetteville St.
D'Orsay—120 S. Mangum St.

BARBER SHOPS
Friendly—711 Fayetteville St.

TAVERNS
Blue Tavern—801 Fayetteville St.
Hollywood—118 S. Mangum St.

SERVICE STATIONS
Granite—Main & 9th St.
Midway—Pine & Poplar Sts.
Pine Street—1102 Pine St.

TAILORS
Union—112 Parrish St.
Royal—538 E. Pettegrew St.

ELIZABETH CITY

TAVERNS
Blue Duck Inn—404½ Ehringhaus

ELIZABETHTOWN

RESTAURANT
Royal Cafe

BEAUTY PARLORS
Liola's Beauty Salon

TAVERNS
Gill's Grill
Royal Cafe

FAYETTEVILLE

HOTELS
Bedford Inn—203 Moore St.
Restful Inn—418 Gillespie St.

TOURIST HOMES
Mrs. L. McNeill—418 Gillespie St.

RESTAURANTS
Mayflower Grill—N. Hillsboro St.

BEAUTY PARLORS
Mrs. Brown—Person St.
Ethel's—Gillespie St.

BARBER SHOPS
DeLuxr—Pesno St.
Mack's—117 Gillespie St.

TAVERNS
Bedford Inn—203 Moore St.
Big Buster—Gillespie St.

SERVICE STATIONS
Moore's—613 Ramsey St.

GARAGES
Jeffrie's—Blount St.

GASTONIA

HOTELS
Union Square

GREENSBORO

HOTELS
Travelers Inn—612 E. Market St.
Legion Club—829 E. Market St.
Dixie—423 Lindsay St.

TOURIST HOMES
T. Daniels—912 E. Market St.
Mrs. E. Evans—906 E. Market St.
Mrs. Lewis—829 E. Market St.
I. W. Wooten—423 Lindsay St.

TAVERNS
Paramount—907 E. Market St.

TAILORS
Shoffners—922 E. Market St.

TAXICABS
MacRae—106 S. Macon St.

GREENVILLE

RESTAURANTS
Paradise—314 Albermale Ave.
Bell's—310 Albermale Ave.

BEAUTY SHOPS
Spain—614 Atlantic Ave.
Midgett's—212 Clark St.

SERVICE STATION
Eagle's

DRUG Stores
Harrison's—908 Dickerson St.

HALLSBORO

BEAUTY PARLORS
Leigh's—Route No. 1

HENDERSON

TAXICABS
Green & Chavis—720 Eaton St.

HIGH POINT

HOTELS
Kilby's—627½ E. Washington St.

LITTLETON

HOTELS
Young's Hotel

MT. OLIVE

RESTAURANTS
Black Beauty Tea Room

NEW BERN

HOTELS
Rhone—42 Queen St.

TOURIST HOMES
H. C. Sparrow—68 West St.

TAVERNS
Palm Garden—192 Broad St.

LEXINGTON

SERVICE STATIONS
D. T. Taylor—Esso Service

RALEIGH

HOTELS
Lewis—220 E. Cabarrus St.
Arcade—122 E. Hargett St.

RESTAURANTS
B & H Cafe—411 S. Blount St.
Chicken Shack—Cross & Lake St.

BEAUTY SHOPS
Sales—222 S. Tarboro St.

TAVERNS
Savoy—410 S. Blount St.
Savoy—410 S. Bount St.

TAXICABS
Capitol—Phone 9137
Hooper's—402½ W. South St.

TAILORS
Peerless—103 W. Jones St.
Provressive—Smithfield & Bloodworth Sts.

GARAGES
Richardson & Smith—108 E. Lenoir St.

PINEHURST

TOURIST HOMES
Foster's

SERVICE STATIONS
Foster's

SANFORD

BEAUTY PARLORS
Douglas'—310 Wall St.

GARAGES
Campbell's—Pearl St.

DRUG STORES
Bland's—300 S. Steele St.

SALISBURY

TAXICABS
Safety—122 N. Lee St.

SUMTER

TAVERNS
Silver Moon—20 W. Liberty St.

WHITEVILLE

TOURIST HOMES
Mrs. F. Jeffries—Mill St.

WILSON

HOTELS
Biltmore—E. Washington St.
The Wilson Biltmore—539 E. Nash

TAXICABS
M. Jones—1209 E. Queen St.

WINDSOR

TOURIST HOMES
W. Payton

WINSTON-SALEM

HOTELS
Y. M. C. A.—410 N. Church St.
Lincoln—9 E. Third St.

TOURIST HOMES
Charles H. Jones—1611 E. 14th St.
Mrs. H. L. Christian—302 E. 9th St
R. B. Williams—1225 N. Ridge Ave.

NIGHT CLUBS
Club 709—709 Patterson Ave.

WASHINGTON

DRUG STORES
Lloyd's—408 Gladden St.

WELDON

HOTELS
Pope
Terminal Inn—Washington Ave.

WILMINGTON

HOTELS
Paynes—417 N. 6th St.
Murphy—813 Castle St.

RESTAURANTS
Harris—10th & Worcester Sts.
Johnson's—1007 Chestnut St.
Hillcrest—1118 Dawson St.
Manhattan—816 S. 13th St.
Ollie's—415½ S. 7th St.

BEAUTY PARLORS
Beth's—416 Anderson St.
Lizora's—609 Red Cross St.
Germany's—715 Red Cross St.
Lou's—830 Red Cross St.
Newkirk's—1217 Castle St.
Pierce's—615 Kidder St.
Apex—613 Red Cross St.
Dickson—1101 S. 7th St.
Gertrude's—415 S. 7th St.
Howard's—121 S. 13th St.
Vanity Box—115 S. 13th St.
La Celeste—508 Nixon St.
La May—703 S. 15th St.
Dixie—512½ Nixon St.

BARBER SHOPS
Johnson's—6 Market St.

NIGHT CLUBS
High Hat—Market St. Rd. (4 miles out)
Del Morocco—1405 Dawson St.

TAVERNS
Happy Hour—6tth & Brunswick Sts.
High Hat—713 Castle St.
Black Cat—922 N. 7th St.
William's—8th & Dawson Sts.
Blinker Cafe—605 Red Cross St.

TAXICABS
Star—601½ Red Cross St.
Mack's—520 N. 7th St.
Dixie—516 S. 7th St.
Blue Bird—517 N. 8th St.
Tom's—418 McRae St.
Crosby's—124 S. 13th St.
Greyhound—Phone 2-1342

OHIO
AKRON

HOTELS
Green Turtle—Federal & Howard
Exchange—32 N. Howard St.
Garden City—Howard & Furnace
Mathews—77 N. Howard St.
The Upperman—197 Bluff St.

TOURIST HOME '
R. Wilson—370 Robert St.

BEAUTY PARLORS
Beauty Salon—70 N. Howard St.

BARBER SHOP
Goodwill's—422 Robert St.
Matthew's—77 N. Howard St.
Allen's—43 N. Howard St.

TAVERNS
Brook's—42 N. Howard St.
Garden City—124 N. Howard St.

NIGHT CLUBS
Cosmopolitan—33½ N. Howard St.

SERVICE STATIONS
Dunagan—834 Rhoades Ave.
Zuber's—47 Cuyhaga St.

ALLIANCE

TOURIST HOMES
Mrs. W. Jackson—774 N. Webb Ave.

CANTON

HOTELS
Phillis Wheatly Asso.—612 Market Ave.

TOURIST HOMES
Smallwood—1203 Housel St. S. W.

RESTAURANTS
Hunters—527 Cherry Ave. S. E.

BEAUTY PARLORS
Vanitie—528 Cherry Ave. S. E.

BARBER SHOPS
Barbes—525 Cherry Ave. S. E.

DRUG STORE
Southside—415 Cherry Ave. S. E.

CINCINNATI

HOTELS
Y. W. C. A.—702 W. 8th St.
Terminal—1103 Hopkins St.
Cotton Club.
Club Tavern—540 W. 7th St.

HOTELS
Sterling—6th & Mound Sts.
Cordella—612 N. 6th St.
Manse—1004 Chapel St.

TOURIST HOMES
O. Steele—3065 Kerper St.

RESTAURANTS
Miniature Grill—1132 Chapel St.
Grand—600 W. Court St.
Kitty Kat—417 W. 5th St.
Ann—503 W. 5th St.
Mom's—6th & John Sts.
Davis—118 Opera Place
Perkins—430 West 5th St.
Loc-Fre—1634 Freeman St.
8-16—816 W. Court St.
Williams—1051 Freeman St.
Hide Away—4th & Smith St.
7th & Mound Sts.

CHINESE RESTAURANTS
Tim Pang—514 W. 6th St.

BEAUTY PARLORS
Efficiency—878 Beecher Street
The Hosmer—920 Churchill Ave.
Poro—1524 Linn Street
Mill's—2639 Park Ave.

BARBER SHOPS
Collegiate—906 Churchill Ave.
Clark's—422 Central
5th Ave.—528 W. 5th Ave.

TAVERNS
Edgemont Inn—2950 Gilbert Ave.
Travelers Inn—1115 Hopkins St.
Log Cabin—608 John Street
Kitty Kat—417 W. 5th St.
Log Cabin—602 John St.

66

DRUG STORES
Sky Pharmacy—5th & John Sts.
Hoard's—937 Central Ave.
Fallon's—6th & Mound Sts.
West End—709 W. Court St.

NIGHT CLUBS
Cotton Club—6th & Mound Street
Cotton Club—6th & Mound St.

ROAD HOUSE
Shuffle Inn—7th & Carr Streets

TAILORS
De Luxe—1217 Linn St.

SERVICE STATIONS
Coursey—Gilbert & Beuna Vista
S. & W.—9th & Mound Sts.
Coursey—2985 Gilbert Ave.

GARAGES
Adams—2915 Gilbert Ave.
7th St.—328 W. 7th St.

TAXICABS
Calvin—9th & Mound St.
Ferguson's—Alma Pl. & Lincoln Ave.

CLEVELAND

HOTELS
Ward—4113 Cedar Ave.
Phyllis Wheatly—4300 Cedar Ave.
Geraldine—2212 E. 40th St.
Y. M. C. A.—E. 76th & Cedar
Majestic—2291 E. 55th St.
Carnegie—6903 Carnegie Ave.

TOURIST HOMES
Mrs. Edith Wilkins—2121 E. 46th St.

RESTAURANTS
Williams—Central & E. 49th St.
Cassie's—2284 E. 55th St.
Manhattan—9903 Cedar Ave.
Cassie's—2284 E. 55th St.
State—7817 Cedar

BEAUTY PARLORS
Cosmetology—Phyllis Wheatly Bldg.
Alberta's—8203 Cedar Ave.
Alberta's—81st & Cedar
Wilkin's—12813 Kinsman Road
Unique De Luxe—2408 E. 79th St.
Parisian—53 N. Howard St.
Poro—48 N. Howard St.
Smart—249 Euclid Ave.
Morris—46 N. Howard St.

BARBER SHOPS
Bryant's—9808 Cedar Ave.
Driskill—1243 E. 105th St.

TAVERNS
Brown Derby—40th & Woodland Ave.
Cedar Gardens—9706 Cedar Ave.
Gold Bar—Massie & E. 105th St.
Log Cabin—2294 E. 55th St.
Cafe Society—966 E. 105th St.
Gold Bar—105th St. & Massie Ave.

NIGHT CLUBS
Douglas—7917 Cedar Ave.

BEAUTY SCHOOLS
Wilkins—2112 East 46th St.

SERVICE STATIONS
Kyer's—Cedar & 79th St.
Douglas—E. 93rd & Cedar Ave.
Wrights Ohio Service—7 Stations
K & R Garfield & E. 105th St.
Amoco—Ashbury & E. 105th St.

GARAGES
Rollin—E. 40th St. & Central
Sykes—13618 Emily Avenue
Ben's—834 E. 105th St.

DRUG STORES
Benjamin's—E. 55th St. & Central

TAILORS
Gant's—10026 Cedar Ave.
Serv-well—1283 E. 105th St.
Primrose—2928 Woodland Ave.
Yale—876 E. 105th St.

COLUMBUS

HOTELS
Madonna Apts.—Tayor & Long St.
Ford—179 N. 6th St.
Lexington—180 Lexington Ave.
Norfolk—430 N. Monroe Ave.
Plaza—Long St. & Hamilton Ave.
Macon Hotel—366 N. 20th St.
Charlton—439 Hamilton Ave.
Flints—703 E. Long St.
Hawkins—65 N. Monroe Ave.
Litchferd—N. 4th St.
Fulton—403 E. Fulton St.

TOURIST HOMES
Hawkins—70 N. Monroe Ave.

RESTAURANTS
Belmont—689 E. Long St.

TAVERNS
Poinciana—758 E. Long St.

NIGHT CLUBS
Club Rogue—772½ E. Long St.
Turf Club—Champion at Mt. Vernon

SERVICE STATIONS
King's—E. Long & Monroe
Peyton Sohio's—E. Long & Monroe

TAILORS
Prince's—677 E. Long St.

DAYTON

HOTELS
Y. M. C. A.—907 W. 5th St.

TOURIST HOMES
B. Lawrence—206 Norwood St.

LIMA

TOURIST HOMES
Sol Downton—1124 W. Spring St.
Edward Holt—406 E. High St.
Amos Turner—1215 W. Spring St.
George Cook—230 S. Union St.

LORAIN

TOURIST HOMES
Mrs. Alex Cooley—114 W. 26th St.
Mrs. W. H. Redmond—201 E. 22nd St.
Worthington—209 W. 16th Stt.
Porter Wood—1759 Broadway
H. P. Jackson—2383 Apple Ave.

MANSFIELD

HOTELS
Lincoln—757 N. Bowman St.

MARIETTA

HOTELS
St. James—Butler St.
TOURIST HOMES
Mrs. E. Jackson—213 Church St.

MIDDLETOWN

RESTAURANTS
Dew Drop Inn—1232 Garfield
BARBER SHOPS
Acme—808 Lincoln Ave.
TAILORS
Tramell—1308 Garfield

OBERLIN

HOTELS
Oberlin Inn—College & Main

SPRINGFIELD

HOTELS
Posey—209 S. Fountain Ave.
Y. M. C. A.—Center St.
Y. W. C. A.—Clarke St.
Burtons—120 Center St.
TOURIST HOMES
Mrs. M. E. Wilborn—220 Fair St.
H. Sydes—902 S. Yellow Spring St.
Mrs. C. Seward—1090 Mound St.
RESTAURANTS
Burton's—642 S. Yellow Spring St.
Mrs. J. Johnson—416 W. Southern
Posey—211 S. Fountain Ave.
Stewart's—217 E. Main St.
BEAUTY PARLORS
Louise—902 Innesfallen Ave.
Powder Puff—638 S. Wittenberg Ave.
BARBER SHOPS
Harris—39 W. Clark Street
Griffith & Martin—127 S. Center St.
TAVERNS
Posey's—211 S. Fountain Ave.
NIGHT CLUBS
K. P. Imp. Club—S. Yellow Spring
SERVICE STATIONS
Underwood-1303 S. Yellow Sp'ng. St.
GARAGES
Green's—1371 W. Pleasant St.
Ben's—935 Sherman Ave.

STEUBENVILLE

TOURIST HOMES
W. Jackson—648 Adam St.
H. Jackson—650 Adam St.

TOLEDO

HOTELS
Y. M. C. A.—669 Indiana Ave.
Pleasant—15 N. Erie Ave.
TOURIST HOMES
G. Davis—532 Woodland Ave.
J. F. Watson—399 Pinewood Ave.
P. Johnson—1102 Collingwood Blvd.
BEAUTY PARLORS
Personality—913 Collingwood Blvd.
BARBER SHOPS
Chiles—Indiana & Collingwood
TAVERNS
Indiana—529 Indiana Ave.
Midway—764 Tecumsik St.
SERVICE STATIONS
Darling's—858 Pinewood Ave.
Hobb's—City Park & Belmont
South—Dorr & City Park

YOUNGSTOWN

HOTELS
Y. M. C. A.—962 W. Federal St.
NIGHT CLUBS
40 Club—399 E. Federal St.

ZANESVILLE

HOTELS
Park—1561 W. Main St.
RESTAURANTS
Little Harlem—Lee St.
TOURIST HOMES
L. E. Coston—1545 N. Main St.
BARBER SHOPS
Nap Love—Second St.
BEAUTY PARLORS
Celeste—South St.

OKLAHOMA

BOLEY

HOTELS
Berry's—South Main St.

CHICKASHA

TOURIST HOMES
Boyd's—1022 Shepard St.

ENID

TOURIST HOMES
Allen Crumb—222 E. Park St.
Mrs. Eliza Baty—520 E. State St.
Mrs. Johnson—217 E. Market St.
Edward's—222 E. Park St.
Vandorf—Broadway & Washington

GUTHRIE

TOURIST HOMES
James—1002 E. Springer Ave.
Mrs. M. A. Smith—317 E. Second St.

MUSKOGEE

HOTELS
Elliot's—111½ S. Second St.
Bozeman
Peoples—316 N. Second St.
RESTAURANTS
Do-Drop Inn—220 S. 2nd St.
BARBER SHOPS
Central—228 N. Second St.
Peoples—312 N. Second St.
Robbins—Second at Court
BEAUTY PARLORS
Pete's—312 N. 2nd St.
TAVERNS
Eagle Bar—Second at Court
Crazy Rock Inn—318 N. Second St.
ROAD HOUSES
Blue Willow Inn—1008 S. 24th St.
SERVICE STATIONS
Smith Tire Co.—2nd at Dennison
GARAGES
Middleton's—420 N. Second St.
Nelson's—940 S. 20th St.
TAILORS
Williams—321 N. 2nd St.
Ezell's—208 S. 2nd St.

OKLAHOMA CITY

HOTELS
Little Page—219 N. Central Ave.
Hall—308½ N. Central
M. & M.—219 N. Central
Magnolia Inn—629 E. 4th
Wilson's—200 N. E. 2nd St.
TOURIST HOMES
COrtland Rms.—629 N. E. 4th
Scrugg's—420 N. Laird St.
Tucker's—315½ N. E. 2nd St.
RESTAURANTS
Eastside Food Shop—904 N. E. 2nd St.
Scales—322 A. N. E. 2nd St.
Ruby—322½ N. E. 2nd St.
King's—905 N. E. 4th St.
BEAUTY PARLORS
Chambers—531 N. Kelly St.
Lyons—316 North Central
N. B. Ellis—331½ N. E. 2nd St.
BARBER SHOPS
Elks—300 Block N. E. 2nd St.
Golden Oak—300 Block N. E. 2nd
Clover Leaf—300 Block N. E. 2nd St.
TAVERNS
Lyons—304 E. 2nd St.
Scales—322A N. E. 2nd St.
Ruby's—322½ N. E. 2nd St.
King's—905 N. E. 4th St.
SERVICE STATIONS
Richardson—400 N. E. 2nd St.
Deep Rock—400 N. E. 2nd St.
Harry"s—547 N. E. 3rd St.
Mathues—1023 N. E. 4th St.

GARAGES
Ed's—220 N. E. 1st St.
DRUG STORES
Randolph—331 N. E. 2nd St.
Cut Rate—301 N. E. 2nd St.

OKMULGEE

RESTAURANTS
Louisiana
Simmons—407 E. 5th St.
BEAUTY PARLORS
Walker—717 N. Porter
SERVICE STATIONS
Phillips—5th & Delaware Sts.
TAXICABS
H. & H.—421 E. 5th St.

SHAWNEE

HOTELS
Olison—501 S. Bell St.
Slugg's—410 So. Bell St.
TOURIST HOMES
M. Gross—602 S. Bell St.

TULSA

HOTELS
Small—615 E. Archer St.
Lincoln—E. Archer St.
Red Wing—206 N. Greenwood
Royal—605 E. Archer St.
McHunt—1121 N. Greenwood Ave.
Warren Hotel
Y. W. C. A.—621 E. Oklahoma Pl.
TOURIST HOMES
W. H. Smith—124½ N. Greenwood
Gentry—537 N. Detroit Ave.
C. LL. Netherland—542 N. Eigin St.
RESTAURANTS
Your Cab—517 E. Beady St.
Barbeque—1111 N. Greenwood Ave.
BEAUTY PARLORS
Cotton Blossom—308 E. Haskell
May's—523 N. Greenwood Ave.
BARBER SHOPS
Swindall's—203 N. Greenwood
SERVICE STATIONS
Mince—2nd & Eigin Sts.
GARAGES
Pine Street—906 E. Pine St.
DRUG STORES
Meharry Drugs—101 Greenwood St.

OREGON

PORTLAND

HOTELS
Medley—2272 N. Interstate Ave.
Y. W. C. A.—N. E. Williams Ave. & Till.

RESTAURANTS
Ballot Box—1504 N. Williams Ave.
Barno's—84 N. E. Broadway St.
Barno's—84 N. E. Broadway
Cozy Inn 66 N. W. Broadway
BEAUTY PARLORS
Bakers—6535 N. E. Grand Ave.
Redmond—2862 S. E. Ankeny
Mott Sisters—2107 Vancouver Ave.
BARBER SHOPS
Holliday's—511 N. W. 6th Ave.
NIGHT CLUBS
Oregon Frat.—1412 N. Wms.
Fraternal Ass'n.—1412 N. William
Avenue
ROAD HOUSE
Spicers—1734 N. Williams Ave.
GARAGE
English—N. E. Williams & Weidler
TAXICABS
Broadway DeLuxe
Phone: BR 1-2-314

PENNSYLVANIA
ALLENTOWN

RESTAURANTS
Southern—372 Union Street
Elsie's—372 Union St.
BEAUTY PARLORS
Baker's—382½ Union St.

ALTOONA

TOURIST HOMES
C. Bell—1420 Wash. Ave.
Mrs. E. Jackson—2138-18th St.
Mrs. H. Shorter—2620-8th St.
RESTAURANTS
Mac's—1710 Union Ave.

BEDFORD

HOTELS
Harris—200 West St.

COATESVILLE

HOTELS
Subway

CHESTER

HOTELS
Harlem—1909 W. 3rd St.
Moonglow 225 Market Street
RESTAURANTS
Rio—321 Central Ave.
BEAUTY PARLORS
Rosella—413 Concord Ave.
Alex. Davis—123 Reaney St.
BARBER SHOPS
Bouldin—1710 W. 3rd St.

TAVERNS
Wright's—3rd St. & Central Ave.
TAILORS
Tailor Shop—601 Tilgaman

DARBY

TAVERNS
Golden Star—10th & Forrester

ERIE

HOTELS
Pope—1318 French Street

GETTYBURG

TOURIST HOMES
Mrs. J. Forsett—210 W. High

GERMANTOWN PHIL

HOTELS
Y. M. C. A.—132 W. Rittenhouse
TOURIST HOMES
M. Foote—5560 Blakmore St.
TAVERNS
Terrace Grill—75 E. Sharpnack St.

GREENSBURG

RESTAURANT
Breeze Inn—618 W. Otterman St.

HARRISBURG

HOTELS
Alexander—7th & Boas Sts.
Jackson—1004 N. 6th St.
Jack's—1208 N. 6th St.
TOURIST HOMES
Mrs. H. Carter—606 Foster St.
Mrs. W. D. Jones—613 Forester St.
BEAUTY PARLORS
Rowland—1321 N. 6th St.
BARBER SHOP
Jack's—1002 N. 6th St.
SERVICE STATION
Broad St.—417 Broad St.

LANCASTER

TOURIST HOMES
E. Clark—449 S. Duke St.
J. Carter—143 S. Duke St.
A. LL. Polite—540 North St.

NEW CASTLE

HOTELS
Y. W. C. A.—140 Elm St.

OIL CITY

TOURIST HOMES
Mrs. Jackson—258 Bissel Ave.
Mrs. M. Moore—8 Bishop St.

PHILADELPHIA

HOTELS
Baltimore—1438 Lombard Street
Attucks—801 S. 15th Street
Elizabeth—756 S. 16th St.
Woodson—17th & Lombard
Gilchriest—319 N. 40 St.
Dixie—606 S. 13th St.
The Grand—420 So. 15th St.
Citizens—420 So. 15th St.
Douglas—Broad & Lombard Sts.
Elrae—805 N. 13th St.
LaSalle—2026 Ridge Ave.
New Roadside—514 S. 15th St.
Paradise—1627 Fitzwater St.
James—2052 Catherine St.
Y. M. C. A.—1724 Christian St.
Y. W. C. A.—1605 Catherine St.
Y. W. C. A.—6128 Germantown Ave.
Horseshoe—12th & Lombard
New Phain—2059 Fitzwater
La Reve—Cor. 9th & Columbia Ave.
Chesterfield—Broad & Oxford St.
Ridge—1610 Ridge Ave.
Bilclore—1432 Catherine St.

RESTAURANTS
Marion's—20th & Bainbridge Sts.
Wilson's—21st & Burke Sts.
Seattle—113 South St.
Trott Inn—5030 Haverford Ave.
Mattie's—4225 Pennsgrove St.
Ruth's—1848 N. 17th St.
Luke & Carl's—3901 N. 17th St.
Cost to Cost—1334 South St.
Brigg's—2510 Ridge Ave.

BEAUTY PARLORS
Effie's—5502 W. Girard Ave.
A. Henson—1318 Fairmont Ave.
Jennie's—1618 French St.
LaSalle—2036 Ridge St.
Lady Ross—718 S. 18th St.
Reynolds—1612 N. 13th St.
Rose's—16th & South St.
F. Franklin—2115 W. York St.
Morton's—17th & Bainbridge
Redmond's—4823 Fairmount Ave.
A. B. Tooks—1913 W. Diamond St.

SCHOOL OF BEAUTY CULTURE
Hill School—3610 Haverford Ave.
Carter's School—1811 W. Columbia Ave.

BARBER SHOPS
S. Jones 2064 Ridge Ave.

TAVERNS
Wander Inn—18th & Federal St.
Musical Bar—9th & Columbia Ave.
Butler's Tavern—17th & Carpenter
Campbell's—18th & South St.
Loyal Grill—16th & South St.
Irene's—2200 Ridge Ave.
Lyons—12th & South St.
Blue Moon—1702 Federal St.
Butler's—2066 Ridge Ave.
Modern—11th & Fitzwater
Cotton Grove—1329 South St.
Wayside Inn—13th & Oxford St.

TAVERNS
Wonder Bar—19th & Montgomery
Lenox—Popular & Jessup Sts.
Fred's—1320 South St.
Preston's—4043 Market St.
Jimmy's—1508 Catherine St.
Casbah—39th & Fairmount St.
Dixon's—19th & Montgomery
Last Word—Haverford & 51st St.
Cathrine's—1350 South St.
Postal Card—1504 South St.
Emerson's—15th & Bainbridge St.
Irene's—2200 Ridge Ave.
Brass Rail—2302 W. Columbia Ave.
Club 421—5601 Wyalusing Ave.

NIGHT CLUBS
Cotton Club—2106 Ridge Ave.
Cafe Society—1306 W. Columbia Ave.
Paradise—Ridge & Jefferson
Crystal Room—1935 W. Columbia Ave.
Progressive—1415 S. 20th St.
Zanzibar—1833 W. Columbia Ave.
Cotton Bowl—Master St. & 13th St.

GARAGES
Bond Motor Service—561 N. 20th St.
Booker Bros.—1811 Fitzwater St.
Garage—5732 Westminister Ave.
Garage—1823 Baingridge St.

SERVICE STATIONS
Dorsey Bros.—2009 Oxford St.

PITTSBURGH

HOTELS
Ave'—1538 Wylie Ave.
Bailey's—1308 Wylie Ave.
Bailey's—1533 Center Ave.
Colonial—Wylie & Fulton St.
Park—2215 Wylie Ave.
Potter—1304 Wylie Ave.
Palace—1545 Wylie Ave.

TOURIST HOMES
Godfrey House—1604 Cliff St.
B. Williams—1537 Howard St.
Mrs. William—5518 Claybourne St.

RESTAURANTS
Scotty's—2414 Center Ave.
Dearling's—2524 Wylie Ave.

READING

TOURIST HOMES
C. Dawson—441 Buttonwood St.

SCRANTON

TOURIST HOMES
Elvira R. King—1312 Linden St.
Mrs. J. Taylor—1415 Penn. Ave.
Mrs. C. Jenkins—610 N. Washington Avenue

SHARON HILL

TAVERNS
Dixie Cafe—Hook Rd.—Howard St.

WASHINGTON
TOURIST HOMES
Richardson—140 E. Chestnut St.
B. T. Washington—32 N. College
RESTAURANTS
W. Allen—N. Lincoln St.
M. Thomas—N. Lincoln St.
BARBER SHOPS
Yancey's—E. Spruce St.
NIGHT CLUBS
Thomas Grill—N. Lincoln St.

WAYNE
NIGHT CLUB
Plantation—Gulf Rd. & Henry Av.

WILLIAMSPORT
TOURIST HOMES
Mrs. Edward Randall—605 Maple St.

WILKES BARRE
HOTELS
Shaw—15 So. State St.

YORK
TOURIST HOMES
Mrs. I. Grayson—32 W. Princess St.

RHODE ISLAND
NEWPORT
TOURIST HOMES
Mrs. F. Jackson—28 Hall Ave.
Mrs. L. Jacgson—35 Bath Road

PROVIDENCE
HOTELS
Biltmore
TOURIST HOMES
Mrs. M. A. Greene—85 Meeting St.
W. W. Joyce—12 Benefit St.
Dinah's—462-4 N. Main St.
Hines—462-4 N. Main St.
TAVERN
Dixieland—1049 Westminster St.
BEAUTY PARLLORS
B. Boyd's—43 Camp St.
Geraldine's—205 Thurbus Ave.
Marie Wells—18 Benefit St.
AUTOMOBILES
George's—203 Plainfield St.

SOUTH CAROLINA
AIKEN
TOURIST HOMES
C. F. Holland—1118 Richland Ave.
M. H. Harrison—Richland Ave.
DRUGGIST
Dr. C. C. Johnson—1432 Park Ave.

BEAUFORD
SERVICE STATIONS
Peoples—D. Brofn, Prop.

CHARLESTON
TOURIST HOMES
Mrs. Gladsen—15 Nassau St.
Mrs. Mayes—82½ Spring St.
L. Harleston—250 Ashley Ave.
A. Serrant—99 Coming St.
TAVERNS
Harleston's—250 Ashley Ave.

COLUMBIA
HOTELS
Y. W. C. A.—1429 Park St.
Taylor—1016 Washington St.
Community Center—831 Hampton St.
TOURIST HOMES
Mrs. S. H. Smith—929 Pine St.
College Inn—1609 Harden Street
Mrs. H. Cornwel—1713 Wayne
Mrs. W. D. Chappelle—1301 Pine St.
Beachum—2212 Gervais Street
Mrs. J. P. Wakefield—1323 Heidt
Mrs. S. H. Smith—929 Pine St.
RESTAURANTS
Green Leaf—1117 Wash. St.
Magnolia—2108 Gervais
Savoy—Old Winnsboro Rd.
Waverly—2315 Gervais St.
White Way—2330 Gervais
Cozy Inn—1509 Harden St.
Mom's—1005 Washington St.
Treye's—2103 Gervais St.
Brown's—1014 Lady St.
BEAUTY PARLORS
Amy's—1125½ Washington St.
Obbie's—1119½ Washington St.
BARBER SHOPS
Holman's—2138 Gervais St.
Stratfords—1003½ Washington St.
Macks—1110 Harden St.
TAVERNS
Taylor's—Broad River Rd.
Mrs. I. Goodum—922 Harden St.
NIGHT CLUBS
Chauffer's—2314 Pendleton
ROAD HOUSES
Macks—1110 Harden St.
SERVICE STATIONS
A. W. Simkins—1331 Park St.
Waverly—2200 Taylor St.
Caldwell's—Oak & Taylor Sts.
GARAGES
Johnson's—1609 Gregg St.
TAXICABS
Blue Ribbon—1072 Washington St.
DRUG STORES
Counts—1105 Washington Street

CHERAW

TOURIST HOMES
Mrs. M. B. Robinson—211 Church St.
Mrs. Maggie Green—Church St.
RESTAURANT
Gate Grill—2nd Street
Watson—2nd Street
TAVERN
College Inn—2nd St.
ROAD HOUSE
Hill Top—Society Hill Road
NIGHT CLUB
Rommie's—High Street
BARBER SHOPS
Imperial—2nd Street
BEAUTY SHOPS
Bell's—Huger St.
SERVICE STATION
Motor Inn—2nd Street

FLORENCE

TOURIST HOMES
Mrs. B. Wright—1004 E. Cheeve St.
J. McDonald—501 S. Irby St.

GEORGETOWN

TOURIST HOMES
Mrs. R. Anderson—424 Broad
Mrs. D. Atkinson—811 Duke
Jas. Becote—118 Orange
T. W. Brown—Merriman & Emanuel
Mrs. A. A. Smith—317 Emanuel

GREENVILLE

HOTELS
Imperial—8 Nelson St.
Liberty—18 Spring St.
TOURIST HOMES
Miss M. J. Grimes—210 Mean St.
Mrs. W. H. Smith—212 John St.
RESTAURANTS
Fowlers—16 Spring St.
BEAUTY PARLORS
Broadway—11 Spring St.
BARBER SHOPS
Broadway—8 Spring St.
DRUG STORES
Gibb's—Broad & Fall St.

MULLENS

HOTELS
283 W. Front St.
Ace Hi—148 Front St.
TOURIST HOMES
E. Calhoun's—535 N. Smith St.
RESTAURANTS
Ace Hi—148 Front St.
BEAUTY PARLORS
Bessie Pitts'—Smith St.
BARBER SHOPS
Noham Ham—Front St.

NIGHT CLUBS
Calhoun Nite Club—535 Smith St.
ROAD HOUSES
Kate Odom—76 H'way
SERVICE STATIONS
Ed. Owins'—Front St.
GARAGES
C. B. Pegues—76 H'way

ORANGEBURG

DRUG STORES
Danzler—121 W. Russell St.

SPARTANBURG

TOURIST HOMES
Mrs. O. Jones—255 N. Dean St.
Mrs. L. Johnson—307 N. Dean
RESTAURANTS
Beatty—N. View
Mrs. M. Davis—S. Wofford
Howard's—415 S. Liberty St.
BEAUTY PARLORS
Harmon—221 N. Dean St.
Callaham—226 N. Dean St.
Clowney's—445 S. Liberty St.
BARBER SHOPS
R. Browning—122 Short Wofford
TAVERNS
Moonlight—N. Vito & Chasander
Victory—Union Highway
NIGHT CLUBS
Club Paradise—491 S. Liberty
SERVICE STATIONS
Collins—398 S. Liberty St.
South Side—S. Liberty St.
Magnolia—217 Magnolia St.
TAXICABS
Collin's—389 S. Liberty St.

SUMTER

TOURIST HOMES
Mrs. Julia E. Byrd—504 N. Main
Edmonia Shaw—206 Manning Ave.
C. H. Bracey—210 W. Oakland
TAVERNS
Steve Bradford—N. Main St.
SERVICE STATIONS
Esso Gas Station
DRUG STORES
Peoples—5 W. Liberty St.

SOUTH DAKOTA

ABERDEEN

HOTELS
Alonzo Ward—S. Main St.
RESTAURANTS
Virginia—303 S. Main St.
BEAUTY PARLORS
Marland—321 S. Main St.

BARBER SHOPS
Olson—103½ S. Main St.
SERVICE STATIONS
Swanson—H'way 12 & Main Sts.
GARAGES
Spaulding—S. Lincoln St.
Wallace—S. Lincoln St.

PIERRE
TOURIST CAMPS
U. S. No. 14 (Inquire)

SIOUX FALLS
TOURIST HOMES
Mrs. J. Moxley—915 N. Main
Chamber of Commerce—131 S. Phillips Ave.
(Inquire)

TENNESSEE
BRISTOL
HOTELS
Palace—210 Front St.
TOURIST HOMES
A. D. Henderson—301 McDowell

CHATTANOOGA
HOTELS
Y. M. C. A.—793 E. 9th St.
Lincoln—1101 Carter St.
Martin—204 E. 9th St.
Peoples—1104 Carter St.
TOURIST HOMES
Mrs. J. Baker—843 E. 8th St.
Mrs. E. Brown—1129 E. 8th St.
Mrs. D. Lowe—803 Fairview Ave.
Y. W. C. A.—839 E. 8th St.
J. Carter—1022 E. 8th St.
RESTAURANTS
Chief—215 W. 9th St.
BEAUTY PARLORS
May's—208 E. 9th Street
SERVICE STATIONS
Mann Bros.—528 E. 9th St.
GARAGES
Volunteer—E. 9th St. & Lindsay
TAXICABS
Simms—915 University Ave.

CLARKSVILLE
HOTELS
Central—535 Franklin St.
RESTAURANTS
Foston's—851 College St.
TOURIST HOMES
Mrs. H. Northington—717 Main St.
Mrs. Kate Stewart—500 Poston St. (Blk)
Black & White—S. Clarksville St.
BARBER SHOPS
Wilson's—900 Franklin St. (Blk).

BEAUTY PARLORS
Johnson's—10th St.
KNOXVILLE
HOTELS
Y. W. C. A.—329 Temperance St.
Brownlow—219 E. Vine St.
Hartford—219 E. Vine St.
TOURIST HOMES
N. Smith—E. Vine St.
Walker's—E. Church St.
LEXINGTON
TOURIST HOMES
C. Timberlake—Holly St.
MEMPHIS
HOTELS
Clarke—144 Beale Ave.
Travelers—347 Vance
Mitchells—160 Hernando St.
Marquette—406 Mulberry St.
RESTAURANTS
The Parkview—516 N. 3rd St.
Bob's—195 S. 3rd St.
Scott's—368 Vance Ave.
Davidson's—345 S. 4th St.
Bessie's—338 Vance Ave.
Moonlight—900 S. Landerdale
BEAUTY PARLORS
Chiles'—341 Beale Ave.
BEAUTY SCHOOLS
Burchitts'—201 Hernando St.
Superior—1550 Florida Ave.
Johnson—316 S. 4th St.
TAILORS
Parks—697 Landerdale
DRUG STORES
So. Memphis—907 Florida Ave.
MURFREESBORO
TOURIST HOMES
Mrs. M. E. Howland—439 E. State
R. Moore—University & State St.
NASHVILLE
HOTELS
Carver—1122 Charlotte Ave.
Y. M. C. A.—4th & Charlotte Aves.
Carver Courts—White's Creek Pike
Y. W. C. A.—436 5th Ave. N.
Bryant—500 8th Ave. S.
Y. M. C. A.—436-5th Ave., N.
Fred Douglas—501 4th Ave. N.
TOURIST HOMES
Mrs. C. James—1902 18th St. N.
BEAUTY PARLORS
Queen of Sheba—1503 14th Ave. N.
Queen of Shebra—1503 14th Ave. N.
Estelle—405 Charlotte Ave.
RESTAURANTS
Dew Drop Inn—2514 Booker St.
Black Hawk—1124 Cedar St.
Martha's—309 Cedar St.

BARBER SHOPS
'Y'—34 4th Ave. N.
BEAUTY PARLORS
Myrtles—2423 Eden St.

TEXAS
ABILENE
TAVERNS
Hammond Cafe—620 Plum St.

AMARILLO
HOTELS
Mayfair—119 Van Buren St.
RESTAURANTS
Murphy Crain—400 W. 3rd St.
BEAUTY PARLORS
Mal-Ber School—116 Harrison St.
ROAD HOUSES
Working Man's Club—202 Harrison

AUSTIN
TOURIST HOMES
Mrs. J. W. Frazier—810 E. 13th St.
Mrs. J. W. Duncan—1214 E. 7th St.
Mrs. W. M. Tears—1203 E. 12th St.
Porter's—1315 E. 12th St.

BEAUMONT
TOURIST HOMES
Mrs. B. Rivers—730 Forsythe St.
RESTAURANTS
Long Bar-B-Q—539 Forsythe St.

CORPUS CHRISTIE
RESTAURANTS
Avalon—1510 Ramirez
Skylark—1216 N. Staples
Liberty—1406 N. Alemeda
Blue Willow—806 Winnebago
Little Aisle—1530 Ramirez
Square Deal—810 Winnebago
Savoy—1007 N. Taneahua
Royal—1222 N. Staples St.
Fortuna—1307 N. Staples St.
BEAUTY PARLORS
Johnson's—1405 Chipito St.
Edna's—921 San Rankin
Just-a-Mere—901 Parker St.
Mitchell's—1519 Ramirez St.
BARBER SHOPS
Steen's—1303 N. Alameda St.
NIGHT CLUBS
Alabam—1503 Ramirez
Elite—1216 N. Staples St.
LIQUOR STORES
Pier—821 Winnebago St.
Savoy—1220 N. Staples St.
TAILORS
Burley's—1223 N. Alameda St.
McIntyre's—1426 Ramirez

CORSICANA
TOURIST HOMES
Rev. Conner—E. 4th Ave.
Robert Lee—712 E. 4th
RESTAURANTS
Early Birds Cafe—220 E. 5th Ave.
BARBER SHOPS
Mrs. Dellum—117 E. 5th Ave.

DALLAS
HOTELS
Grand Terrace—Boll & Juliett
Lewis—302½ N. Central St.
Powell—3115 State St.
Y. M. C. A.—2700 Flora St.
Y. W. C. A.—3525 State St.
Hall's—1825½ Hall St.
Lone Star—3118 San Jacinto St.
RESTAURANTS
Beaumont Barbeque—1815 Orange
Tommie & Fred's—Washington & Thomas A.
Davis—6806 Lemmon Ave.
Palm Cafe—2213 Halls St.
BEAUTY PARLORS
S. Brown's—1721 Hall St.
BARBER SHOPS
Washington's—3203 Thomas Ave.
TAVERNS
Hall St.—1804 Hall St.
NIGHT CLUBS
Regal—3216 Thomas Ave.
GARAGES
Givens—2201 Leonard Ave.
DRUG STORE
Smith's—2221 Hall St.

EL PASO
HOTELS
Hotel Murray—214-224 S. Mesa Ave.
Phillips Manor—704 S. Vrain St.
Jordan's—104 Kemp St.
Daniel Hotel—413 S. Oregon St.
TOURIST HOMES
A. Winston—3205 Almeda St.
Mrs. S. W. Stull—511 Tornillo
C. Williams—1507 Wyoming St.
L. Walker—2923 E. San Antnio
E. Phillips—704 S. St. Vrain St.
TAVERNS
Daniel's—403 S. Orange St.
DRUG STORES
Donnel—3201 Nanzana St.

FORT WORTH
HOTELS
Del Rey—901 Jones St.
Jim—413-15 E. Fifth St.
TOURIST HOMES
Evan's—1213 E. Terrell St.

75

RESTAURANTS
Y. M. C. A.—1604 Jones St.
Green Leaf—315 E. 9th St.
BEAUTY PARLORS
Dickerson's—1015 E. Rosedale
SERVICE STATIONS
South Side—1151 New York St.

GALVESTON

HOTELS
Oleander—421½ 25th St.
RESTAURANT
Mitchell's—417 25th St.
TOURIST HOMES
G. H. Freeman—1414 29th St.
Mrs. J. Pope—2824 Ave. M
Cotton's—2907 Ave. L
TAVERNS
Gulf View—28th & Blvd. Houston

HOUSTON

HOTELS
Y. M. C. A.—1217 Bagby St.
Y. W. C. A.—506 Louisiana St.
Cooper's—1011 Dart St.
Dowling—3111 Dowling St.
RESTAURANTS
Eva's—1617 Dowling St.
BEAUTY PARLORS
School & Parlor—222 W. Dallas
Lou Lillie's—2714 Lee St.
BARBER SHOP
—Harris—508 Louisiana St.
TAVERNS
Welcome Cafe—2409 Pease Ave.
LIQUOR STORE
Joe's—2506 Posto....ce
DRUG STORES
Langford's—3026 Pierce St.
Lion's—618 Prarie & Louisiana

MARSHALL

TOURIST HOMES
Rev. Bailey—1103 W. Grand Ave.

MEXIA

HOTELS
Carleton—1 W. Commerce St.
RESTAURANTS
Mrs. M. Carroll—109 N. Belknap St.
BEAUTY PARLORS
Mrs. B. Smith—N. Denton
BARBER SHOPS
Mr. C. Carter—N. Belknap
TAVERNS
R. Houston—N. Belknap
NIGHT CLUBS
Payne's—West Side
ROAD HOUSES
Jim Ransom—N. Carthage

SERVICE STATIONS
Joe Brooks—107 N. Belknap
GARAGES
Rev. T. Sparks—N. Belknap

MIDLAND

HOTELS
Watson's Hotel
Nuf Sed—Moody Addition
RESTAURANTS
King Sandwich—Moody Addition
BEAUTY PARLORS
Beauty Shop Jeanettt
Manbd-Nuf Sed—Moody Addition
BARBER SHOPS
James Moore's—Moody Addition
SERVICE STATIONS
Buster & Bates—Moody Addition
TAXICABS
Johnnie's—Moody Addition

PARIS

HOTELS
Brownrigg—88 N. 22nd St.
TOURIST HOMES
Mrs. I. Scott—405-2nd St., N. E.
Mrs. I. Scott—115 N. 22nd St.

PITTSBURG

TOURIST HOMES
Bobbie's Place—Happy Hollow
S. E. Crawford—Happy Hollow

SAN ANTONIO

HOTELS
Dunbar
TOURIST HOMES
Mundy—129 N. Mesquite St.
RESTAURANTS
Cactus—524 E. Commerce St.
Houston's—318 Hedges St.
Rick's—602 S. Olive St.
Mamie's—1833 E. Houston St.
BEAUTY SHOPS
Optimistic—107 Anderson St.
Jones—209 N. Swiss St.
Band Box—135 N. Mesquite St.
Mitts—115 N. Swiss St.
Arritha's—113 Alabama St.
R & B—126 N. Mesquite St.
Hick's—1515 E. Houston St.
Briscoe's—518 S. Pine St.
Three Point—716 Virginia Blvd.
NIGHT CLUBS
Wood Lake Country Club—New Sulphur
  Spring Road
Zanzibar—108 N. Center St.
Eldorado—1918 Wyoming St.
LIQUOR STORES
Good's—106 Pearl St.
SERVICE STATIONS
Eason's—1605 E. Houston
Mitchell's—805 S. Hackberry St.

TYLER

TOURIST HOMES
Mrs. Thomas—516 N. Border St.
W. Langston—1010 N. Border

TEXARKANA

RESTAURANTS
Casino—504 West 3rd Street
TAVERNS
Dutahess Tea Room—1115 Capp St.
GARAGES
Carl Hill—925 W. 20th St.

WACO

TOURIST HOMES
B. Ashford—902 N. 8th St.
RESTAURANTS
Kirk's—1114 S. First St.
Harlem—123 Bridge
Ideal—109 N. 2nd St.
ROAD HOUSE
Golden Lilly—426 Clifton
TAVERN
Green Tree—1325 S. 4th St.
BARBER SHOP
Jockey Club—2nd & Franklin St.
BEAUTY PARLORS
Cendivilla—107½ N. Second St.
Cinderella—1133 Earle St.
Ideal—1029 Taylor St.
Earle St.—1113 Earle St.
Mayfair—112 Bridge St.
Modern—1406 Taylor St.
Hine's—1125 Earle St.
Murphy's—115 So. 2nd St.
SERVICE STATION
Hick's—2nd & Franklin St.
GARAGE
Malone—Clay & River St.

WAXAHACHIE

TOURIST HOMES
Mrs. A. Nunn—413 E. Main St.
Mrs. M. Johnson—427 E. Main St.
Mrs. N. Lowe—418 E. Main St.
Mrs. N. Jones—430 E. Main St.

WICHITA FALLS

HOTELS
Bridges—404 Sullivan St.
TOURIST HOMES
E. B. Jeffrey—509 Juarez St.
T. S. Jackson—Park St.

UTAH

SALT LAKE CITY

HOTELS
New Hotel J. H.—250 West So. Temple

VERMONT

BURLINGTON

HOTELS
The Pates—86-90 Archibald St.
TOURIST HOMES
George E. Braxton—191 Champlain St.
Mrs. William Sharper—242 North St.
SERVICE STATIONS
McDermotts Esso Station

MANCHESTER

HOTELS
Clyde Blackwells

RUTLAND

TOURIST HOMES
J. H. Meade—83 Strongs Ave.

NORTHFIELD

TOURIST HOMES
Mrs. A. J. Cole—7 Sherman Ave.

VIRGINIA

ABINGTON

TOURIST HOMES
H. Anderson—Near Fairgrounds E. End
Mrs. N. Brown—High St.

ALEXANDRIA

TOURIST HOMES
J. T. Holmes—803 Gibbon St.
J. A. Barrett—724 Gibbon St.

BUCKROE BEACH

HOTELS
Bay Shore
NIGHT CLUBS
Club 400

CARET

TAVERNS
Sessons Tavern

CHARLOTTESVILLE

TOURIST HOMES
Virginia Inn—W. Main St.
Chauffeur's Rest—129 Preston Ave.
Alexander's—413 Dyce St.
BEAUTY PARLORS
Apex—211 W. Main St.
BARBER SHOPS
Jokers—North 4th St.

CHRISTIANBURG

HOTELS
Eureka

DANVILLE

TOURIST HOMES
Yancey's—320 Holbrook Street
Mrs. M. K. Page—434 Holbrook St.
Mrs. S. A. Overby—Holbrook St.

DUNBARTON

TOURIST HOMES
H. Jackson—Route No. 1, Box 322

FARMVILLE

TOURIST HOMES
Wiley's—626 S. Main St.
RESTAURANTS
Reid's—236 Main Street
TAVERNS
Ried's—200 Block, Main St.
SERVICE STATIONS
Clark's—Main Street

FREDERICKSBURG

HOTELS
McGuire—521 Princess Ann St.
Rappahannock—520 Princess St.

HAMPTON

RESTAURANTS
Paul's—216 W. King St.
BARBER SHOP
Paul's—154 Queen St.
BEAUTY PARLORS
Tillie's—215 N. King St.
SERVICE STATION
Lyle's—40 Armitsead Ave.
GARAGES
Walton's—W. Mallory Ave.

HARRISONBURG

RESTAURANTS
Frank's—145 E. Wolf St.

LEXINGTON

TOURIST HOMES
The Franklin—9 Tucker St.
RESTAURANTS
Washington—16 N. Main St.
TAVERNS
Rose Inn—351 N. Main St.

LURAY

TOURIST HOMES
Camp Lewis Mountain—Skyline Drive

LYNCHBURG

HOTELS
Phyllis Wheatley YWCA—613 Monroe Street
Manhattan—1001 Fifth St.
Petersburg—66 Ninth St.
TOURIST HOMES
Mrs. C. Harper—1109 8th St.
Mrs. M. Thomas—919 Polk St.
Mrs. Smith—504 Jackson
Happyland Lake—812 5th Ave.
BEAUTY PARLORS
Selma's—1002 5th St.

SERVICE STATIONS
United—1016 Fifth St.

NATURAL BRIDGE

TOURIST HOMES
Mountain View Cottage

NEWPORT NEWS

TOURIST HOMES
Mrs. W. E. Barron—2123 Jefferson
Mrs. W. R. Cooks—221 Marshall Ave.
Thomas E. Reese—636-25th St.
TOURIST HOMES
Mrs. W. Herndon—752 26th St.
Mrs. C. Stephents—1909 Marshall Ave .
J. H. Tallaferro—2206 Marshall Ave.
RESTAURANTS
Tavern Rest—2108 Jefferson
BEAUTY PARLORS
Rattrie's—300 Chestnut St.
SERVICE STATION
Ridley's—Orcutt Ave. & 30th St.

NORFOLK

HOTELS
Prince George—1757 Church St.
Y. M. C. A.—729 Washington Ave.
Ambrose—616 Brambleton Ave.

TOURIST HOMES
Mrs. S. Noble—725 Chaple St.

BEAUTY PARLORS
Jordan's—526 Brambleton Ave.
Vel-Ber St. Ann—1008 Church St.
Yeargen's—1685 Church St.

TAVERNS
Peoples—Church & Calvert Sts.
Russell's—835 Church St.
SERVICE STATIONS
Alston's—Cor. 20th & Church St.
Mac's—1625 Church St.

PETERSBURG

HOTELS
The Walker House—116 South

PHONE: CHESTER 3953

◆

COLBROOK INN

Rest In Home Surroundings

◆

GOOD FOOD

COMFORTABLE CABINS

◆

U. S. HIGHWAY NO. 1

8 Mi. N. of Petersburg

15 Mi. S. of Richmond

—◆—

W. E. BROOKS, Mgr.

NIGHT CLUBS
Chatter Boy—143 Harrison St.

PHOEBUS

BARBER SHOPS
118 S. Mallory St.

RICHMOND

HOTELS
Slaughters—514 N. 2nd St.
Harris—200 E. Clay St.
Eggleston (Miller's)—2nd & Leigh St.
TOURIST HOMES
Mrs. E. Brice—14 W. Clay St.
Y. W. C. A.—515 N. 7th St.
Jack's—on Rt. No. 1-6 m. N. of Richmond
RESTAURANTS
Cora's—427 E. Leigh St.

BEAUTY PARLORS
Rest-a-Bit—619 N. 3rd St.
BARBER SHOPS
Wright's—412 E. Leigh St.
Scotty's—505 N. 2nd St.
TAVERNS
Market Inn—Washington Park
NIGHT CLUBS
Terrace Club—1212 N. 26th St.
SERVICE STATIONS
Cameron's—Brook Ave. & W. Clay St.
Harris—400 N. Henry St.
Little Lord's—410 N. 2nd St.
Adam St.—523 N. Adams St.

ROANOKE

HOTELS
Dumas—Henry St. N. W.
TOURIST HOMES
Y. M. C. A.—23 Wells Ave. N. W.
Y. W. C. A.—208 2nd St. N. W.
TAVERNS
Tom's Place
F & G—114 N. Henry St.
GARAGES
Maple Leaf—High St. at Henry

SOUTH HILL

HOTELS
Brown's—Melvin Brown, Prop.
Groom's—John Groom, Prop.

STAUNTON

TOURIST HOMES
Pannell's Inn—613 N. Augusta St.
F. T. Jones—515 Baptist St.
RESTAURANTS
Johnson's—301 N. Central Ave.

TAPPAHANNOCK

HOTELS
McGuire's Inn—Marsh St.
TOURIST HOMES
Way Side Inn—Main St.

WARRENTON

RESTAURANTS
Bill's—5th Street
Phil's—5th Street
TOURIST HOMES
Lawson—227 Alexanderia Pike
BARBER SHOPS
Walker's—5th Street
BEAUTY PARLORS
Fowlers—123 N. 3rd St.
TAXICABS
Joyner's—Phone 292
Bland—Phone 430
Parker's—Phone 491

WINCHESTER

HOTELS
Evans—224 Sharp St.

TOURIST HOMES
Mrs. Joe Willis—N. Main St.
Dunbar Tea Room—21 W. Hart St.

RESTAURANTS
Ruth's—128 E. Cecil Street

WASHINGTON

EVERETT

TOURIST HOMES
J. Samuels—2214 Wedmore Ave.
Mrs. J. T. Payne—2912 Pacific
Mrs. G. Samuels—3620 Hoyt Ave.

SEATTLE

HOTELS
Atlas—420 Maynard St.
Y. W. C. A.—102-21 North St.
Green—711 Lane St.
Idaho—505 Jackson St.
Olympus—413 Maynard St.
Dunbar—328 N. W. 5th St.
Eagle—408½ Main St.

RESTAURANTS
Evelyn Inn—2229 E. Madison Ave.
Palm Garden—1040 Jackson St.
Pacific—417 Maynard St.
Paramount—518 Jackson St.
Egyptian—2040 E. Madison St.
Elite—428 - 21st Street
Shanty Inn—110 12th Ave.
Sid's—2330 E. Madison Ave.
Cozy Inn—66 N. E. Broadway
Victory—652 Jackson St.

ROAD HOUSE
Rendezvous—Empire Highway 2½ Mile S.

BEAUTY PARLORS
Pauline's—2221 E. Madison
Modernistic—674 Jackson St.
Streamline—1212 Jackson St.
LaMode—2036 E. Madison St.
Bert's—2301 E. Denny Way
Ruth Whiteside—614 Jackson

BARBER SHOPS
Hayes—2227 E. Madison St.
Stockards—2032 E. Madison St.

NIGHT CLUBS
Playhouse—1238 Main St.

LIQUOR STORES
Jackson's—707 Jackson Street

TAVERNS
Stoemer—2047 E. Madison St.
Hill Top—1200 Jackson St.
Sea Gull—673 Jackson St.
Pacific Cafe—417 Maynard St.
Lucky Hour—1315 Yesler Way

SERVICE STATIONS
Richfield—707 Jackson
Bob's—19th & E. Madison St.
Burnham's—2211 E. Madison St.
Moszee—19 E. Madison St.

DRUG STORES
Bon-Rot—14th & Yesler St.
Bishop's—507 Jackson St.
Chikata—114 12th Ave.
Madison—22nd & Madison

TAILORS
Gilt Edge—611 Jackson St.

TACOMA

TOURIST HOMES
Mrs. A Robinson—1906 S. "I" St.
J. H. Carter—1017 S. Trafton St.

BEAUTY PARLORS
Catherine's—1408 South "K" St.

YAKIMA

TOURIST HOMES
H. C. Deering—508 S. Third St.
Mrs. W. H. Jones—310 Third Ave.

WEST VIRGINIA

BECKLEY

HOTELS
New Pioneer—340 S. Fayette St.

TOURIST HOMES
Mrs. E. Morton—430 S. Fayette St.

RESTAURANTS
Home Service—338½ S. Fayette St.

BEAUTY PARLORS
Katie's Vanity—S. Fayette St.
Fuqua's—Fuqua Bldg. S. Fayette

BARBER SHOPS
Paynes—338 S. Fayette St.
Simpson's—New Pioneer Hotel

NIGHT CLUBS
Beckino Club—S. Fayette St.
Chesterfield Club—New Pioneer Hotel

SERVICE STATIONS
Moss—501 South Fayette Street

DRUG STORES
Morton Drug—S. Fayette St.

TAXICABS
Robertson's—Dial 6542
Nuway—Dial 3301

BLUEFIELD

TOURIST HOMES
Traveler's Inn—602 Raleigh St.

CHARLESTON

HOTELS
Ferguson

TAVERNS
White Front—1007 Washington St.
Palace Cafe—910 Washington St.

HUNTINGTON

HOTELS
The Ross House—911-8th Ave.
Southern—921 8th Ave.
Massey's—837 7th Ave

TOURIST HOMES
Mrs. R. J. Lewis—1412 10th Ave.
Mrs. C. J. Barnett—810 7th Ave.

RESTAURANTS
J. Gross—839 7th Ave.

BEAUTY PARLORS
Louise's—821 19th St.

TAVERNS
Monroe's—1616 8th Ave.
The Alpha—1624 8th Ave.

SERVICE STATIONS
Sterling—Cor. 12th St. & 3rd Ave.

GARAGE
South Side—716 8th Ave.

PARKERSBURG

NIGHT CLUBS
American Legion—812 Avery St.

WELCH

HOTELS
Capehart—14 Virginia Ave.

WHEELING

TOURIST HOMES
Mrs. W. Turner—114 12th St.
Mrs. C. Early—132 12th St.
R. Williams—1007 Chapline St.

RESTAURANTS
Singelery—1043 Chapline St.

BEAUTY PARLORS
Miss Hall—Chapline St.
Miss Taylor—Chapline St.

NIGHT CLUBS
American Legion—1516 Main St.
Elks Club—1010 Chapline St.

WHITE SULPHUR SPRINGS

TOURIST HOMES
Brook's—138 Church Street
Haywood Place—Church St.

WISCONSIN

FOND DU LAC

TOURIST HOMES
Mrs. E. Pirtle—45 E. 11th St.
V. Williams—97 S. Seymour St.

OSHKOSH

TOURIST HOMES
L. Shadd—37 King St.
F. Pemberton—239 Liberty St.

WYOMING

CASPER

TOURIST HOMES
Mrs. J. E. Edwards—347 N. Grant
H. Keeling—331 N. Grant
G. Anderson—320 N. Lincoln St.

CHEYENNE

HOTELS
Barbeque Inn—622 W. 20th St.

TOURIST HOMES
Mrs. L. Randall—612 W. 18th St.

RAWLING

YELLOW FRONT

111 EAST FRONT ST.

See The Golden West

Barbeque Served Every Day

Phone: 1195W

Robert Westbrook, Mgr.

ROCK SPRINGS

TOURIST HOMES
Mrs. R. Collins—915 7th St.

More special edition reprinted books
from New York History Review

A Brief History of Chemung County, New York, 1779 -1905
by Ausburn Towner with new index

Harper's New York & Erie Railroad Guide Book of 1851

The Elmira Prison Camp
by Clay Holmes

Our Own Book : A Victorian Guide To Life

Historical Sketch of the Chemung Valley, New York
by T. Apoleon Cheney

A Soldier's Story
by Miles O. Sherrill

Diary of a Tar Heel Confederate Soldier
by Louis Leon

Zim's Foolish History of Elmira
by Eugene Zimmerman

The Great Inter-State Fair

www.ingramcontent.com/pod-product-compliance
Lightning Source LLC
Chambersburg PA
CBHW061415090426
42742CB00026B/3477